Betty 98

MW00983457

COLLECTOR'S GUIDE TO

DON WINTON

DESIGNS

IDENTIFICATION & VALUES

Michael L. Ellis

Don Winton working at his bench in 1954.

COLLECTOR BOOKS
A Division of Schroeder Publishing Co., Inc.

Searching for a Publisher?

We are always looking for knowledgeable people considered to be experts within their fields. If you feel that there is a real need for a book on your collectible subject and have a large comprehensive collection, contact Collector Books.

Cover design: Beth Summers
Book design: Sherry Kraus

Additional copies of this book may be ordered from:

COLLECTOR BOOKS
P.O. Box 3009
Paducah, Kentucky 42002–3009

@ $19.95. Add $2.00 for postage and handling.

CONTENTS

DON'S TESTIMONY

Monday February 17, 1997

As I look back over the years I can't help but reflect on what an incredible journey we have taken.

From an early age I realized I'd been given a talent to create things out of clay. I freely acknowledge that this was a God given gift.

If there is anything noteable that I have accomplished over the many years I have been active, I give God the credit, and the faithfulness of a Godly mother and wife, Norma. I must also be greatful to friends who introduced me to a man named Bill Bright, president of Campus Crusade for Christ who gently asked me if I was a Christian. When I replied, "I think so," he said "Do you want to make sure?" I said "yes" and he took me up to his study and showed me the plan of salvation from the Bible and I asked Jesus Christ to forgive my sins and take over my life. This encounter with the living Lord changed my life forever and it has been an on going experience and has enriched my life.

I have been blessed beyond measure and Norma and I have shared in this new life in Christ with Him in the center! To God be the Glory!

Don Winton

ACKNOWLEDGMENTS

The acknowledgment of a man for a lifetime of creativity and the people who are his friends, family, and collectors of his work is one in which I dare not start stating names. If even one person got left out, it would be a tragedy because they have all contributed to Don's life and therefore to this book. So from the bottom of my heart, I say thank you.

INTRODUCTION

From the first time I met Don Winton, I have been continually amazed at his genius and God-given ability. His start as a child making colorful bricks on his mom's dining room table to a man who sits with presidents and nobility remind me to never doubt the potential of any individual. The beauty of Don's designs is that no matter how little room you have or the budget you have to start your collection, you can find something that will bring a smile to your face and delight to your heart. The key to collecting his creations is knowing how to recognize his designs. The value of any piece is determined by the seller and you, the collector.

The thing that amazes me about this whole collecting phenomenon is the wonderful preservation of history that all of us share.

I had never heard of Don Winton until 1991, or so I thought. I did not know about the Twin Winton history or that this man is a world class sculptor and artist. I certainly did not think I had any of his pieces. Then I got to know him as a friend and found out I certainly had known him for a very long time through his creations. In 1972 my sister bought some of the Twinton figurines for her apartment. My wife and I were given an Elephant cookie jar for our wedding in 1974. I found that some of the trophies and awards my children had received through the years were designed by Don. It seemed every time Don came to my house he recognized something else I had on display that he created. As you look through this book you will recognize pieces you have at home that Don designed. He did not personally manufacture each item, but his designs are part of our history and will continue to be a part of our lives well into the twenty-first century.

DON WINTON "THIS IS YOUR LIFE"

Don Winton's story begins in Canada on June 2, 1919. He and his twin brother were born to Alice Georgene (Cantelo) Winton and Harry Johnson Winton. They weighed in at a healthy 8 pounds each.... Poor Mom! He had one brother, Bruce, who was four years older. His dad was a pharmacist and worked long hours putting food on the

Dad – Harry Johnson Winton
(Pictured here with Bruce Winton - 1915)

Mom — Alice Georgene (Cantelo) Winton

table. His mom stayed at home and worked long hours raising these three rambunctious boys.

The boys proved to be more than a handful for their mom. One day while older brother Bruce was at school, Mom decided she had to do something to channel the energy of these two active twin boys she still had at home. She went to the Govan Saskatchewan General Store and bought several boxes of oil clay. She sat the twins down and told them to do something with the clay. Mom had no idea she was deciding in 1924 what the boys would do for the rest of their lives. In fact, Don says today, "I knew since I was 5 that I wanted to be a sculptor. I just always loved working with clay and molding things."

Bruce & Ross at play, age 5 (1924)
"Watch that pointy stick, Don!"

The boys were fascinated with the different colors and began to form things like eggs and bricks. They made the colored bricks into a little house, then pro gressed from that to a train, which they modeled on the table of a dining car coming across the Canadian Rockie in 1925. They were on their way to California. The passengers on the train were quite impressed as these tw identical twins fashioned in clay the locomotive and cars in which they were traveling. They were quite a pai No one could tell them apart except for the fact that Ross was right handed and Don was left handed. They wer troublesome treasures to their mom and dad, but never a dull moment. They landed in San Mateo, California where they stayed for two years. At age seven, Ross and Don were given a thick encyclopedia which the devoured. They loved the pictures of animals, which they modeled in clay.

When they settled in Los Angeles in 1927, they lived two blocks from a church named Angelus Temple. The twin boys, true to style, became well known to the congregation when they modeled most of the animals described in the Bible, in full color. Mom bought them a few more pounds of clay for this project. In fact this is where Don and Ross had their first art show. They designed some of the figures from the last book of the Bible, Revelations. These were displayed in the church gift store for a period of time. It so inspired the twins that they decided they wanted to be evangelists. These ambitions changed as they moved on to Pasadena.

Age 12 proved to be a very high and a very low year in the lives of these young artists. These boys had such a high level of energy and creativity that they designed a model of a Chinese settlement while going to junior high. Don made a bust of George Washington that was so good for his age that it was displayed as part of the Centennial Exhibit in the Smithsonian Institute. He recalled a letter from Sol Bloom, an assistant to President Franklin Delano Roosevelt, congratulating him on his talent.

These industrious twins also got permission to put on plays in the school auditorium. There were about 10 kids, all hand picked by Don and Ross. They must have been good at casting because one of their "bit" players named Billy Beadle was discovered by a Hollywood talent scout and became William Holden.

Tragedy struck in the middle of all of the wonderful excitement of being 12 years old. Alice Georgene Winton died of chronic bronchitis. She was a godly woman who was the spiritual head of their family and a devoted wife and mother. She had held the family together, as Harry (Dad) was an alcoholic who had a hard time keeping a job. Her death changed the lives of the boys forever.

Dad and the boys moved back to Pasadena after this and at 14 started John Muir Technical High School. The boys plunged into athletics and really enjoyed the three sports they were involved with, football, track, and basketball. It seems that Don always had as friends those destined for greatness. One of his team mates in high school athletics was the talented Jackie Robinson. The boys gave up sculpting for three years and it wasn't until their senior year that they started again...as a necessity.

They Think, Work Alike

DONALD (LEFT) AND Ross Winton, 12 year-old twins, and model of Chinese Settlement at Shanghai they fashioned from clay. Both hope to become sculptors, working together.
—Examiner photo

Don and Ross at age 12. Pictured here with the model of a Chinese settlement at Shanghai they fashioned from clay.

Don and Ross in high school.
Can you tell the difference?

These wonderful old photos show an example of the very earliest Don Winton designs.

While a junior at John Muir High School the three brothers started making and selling ceramic figures similar to Disney characters. Don says, "We manufactured a variety of cute little cartoon-like animals using the Disney principles of structuring, round circles for the heads and bodies." By the twins' senior year in high school they had a very profitable business going. So profitable, in fact, that Disney management felt threatened. They received a letter from some very angry Disney people telling them to cease and desist. Somehow, Walt Disney heard of their plight, two teenage school kids trying to make a living, and told his attorneys to leave them alone. "Although I never met him, Walt was very supportive. I'll always be grateful for that," says Don as he thinks about those early days.

In his senior year of high school Don started working for a gift shop at Busch Gardens, a popular tourist spot in Southern California. He started making Garden Gnomes for the gift shop. They were full-sized gnomes about 2½ feet tall. He only made about 24 of the large gnomes during his time there because each one was an original sculpture. He also did smaller gnomes on ashtrays and bookends. In 1937, Don and Ross formed their own company jointly with the gift shop lady whose name was Helen Burke. Thus the name Burke-Winton. The boys worked at manufacturing the pieces and Helen worked at decorating them. In 1938 the twins broke away from Helen and formed their own company, Twin Winton Studios. They leased a small industrial building approximately 1400 square feet in Tujunga, California. During this time they mostly manufactured a small line of animals. They made small squirrels, chipmunks, and bunnies, all three to four inches high. Then they brought some larger sizes into the line, up to eight inches tall. The larger ones were quite popular but limited in production because of the space they took in the kiln firing. These would be dated from about 1938 to 1941.

"All our animals were happy little creatures," says Don. They soon outgrew the small industrial space and moved to a 5000 square feet building on Hill Street near Washington in Pasadena.

Don Winton at age 18 about the time he was working at Busch Gardens. Pictured here working on a self portrait and one of the garden gnomes.

In 1942, Don and Ross enlisted for military service and all operations and manufacturing were suspended for the duration of World War II. The boys were all Canadian citizens still because their dad had never taken out citizenship papers. In 1942 older brother, Bruce, became a citizen and applied for flying cadet training in the U.S. Army Corp. After getting his wings and marrying a beautiful blonde named Margaret (Sistie) Tweed, he was shipped overseas to England where he flew B-17s over Germany. He completed 30 missions and distinguished himself as a captain through very hazardous missions, receiving combat medals for his commendable service. Ross was assigned to Signal Corps and was in combat in Europe with General Patton. Don was in the Army Air Corp. After completing officer training, he played football for a service team and was charged with physically conditioning bomber crews. Both Ross and Bruce came back unscathed! After reading a flight log compiled by Bruce's tail gunner, Don concluded that the carnage Bruce's crew went through would make the "Memphis Belle" mission look like a Sunday school picnic.

Don served his time in the armed forces playing football and training bomber crews in physical conditioning.

Don is hard at work in the small factory in So. Pasadena.

Don and Ross standing in front of the shop at 811 Fairview Ave. in So. Pasadena. They were there between 1946 and 1950.

When Don was discharged in late 1946 he returned to Pasadena and the family business. He was 27 years old at the time and single. He had continued perfecting his sculpting skills and convinced the Tournament of Roses committee that he was the man to sculpt a bust of the Rose Queen. What better way to meet one of the most beautiful women in the world.

Don recalls, "After seeing a picture of 100 lovely contestants, I offered to sculpt the winner of the 1947 Rose Queen title. I picked the one I thought would win—actually hoped would win! As the weeks went by, the candidates were narrowed to seven and my pick was among the finalists."

"My choice, Norma, a beautiful, petite blonde, did indeed become the Rose Queen of 1947 and Mrs. Don Winton in 1948," says Don. You sly dog! What did Norma's parents think about this older man dating their 18-year-old daughter. Norma's mom said, "He would be a good catch." After the wedding Don and Norma appeared on a T V game show called BRIDE AND GROOM.

Norma Christopher 1947 Rose Queen posing for Don Winton. I wonder if Norma knew what Don had in mind when she posed for this sculpture.

Mrs. Don Winton recalls 1947, when she was Rose Queen Norma Christopher and Bob Hope was grand marshal.

They were successful and won an all expense paid trip to Sun Valley for their honeymoon. Don almost wound up in the hospital when he attempted to go down suicide run. After all this was his first time skiing! He flopped 10 times on his way down and decided that he should not try the advanced Olympic ski run until he learned how to ski.

Grand marshal of the Rose Parade that year was Bob Hope. Hope and the newlyweds became good friends and Norma says, "When we married, Bob gave us a lovely silver punch bowl and matching candelabra." Don says, "We lost touch over the years, so was pleased when I was commissioned by the Sahara Hotel in Las Vegas to do a statue of him dressed in Army fatigues and carrying a golf club."

In early 1947 the Winton boys came out with th very successful Hillbilly Line. This was inspired by th Paul Webb cartoon series. The line consisted of pitche and mug sets, pretzel bowls, salt & pepper shakers lamps, ashtrays, and other novelty items. The line fea tured figures of the Ozark mountain men and women i

Queen Norma Christopher and her court in 1947 Rose Parade.

different hand-painted colors against a simulated wood grain finish.

This Hillbilly fad lasted about three years until 1950 and they started looking for ways to expand their bus ness. They then started making small figures of children, Godey figures, and developed cookie jars and househol items. In 1952 the twins decided to sell their interest in the business to older brother Bruce. At this point Ro

Pictured here is part of the Hillbilly Line that was popular from 1947 to 1950.

did not have anything further to do with the Twin Winton factory. Don continued designing on a free-lance basis as the only designer for Twin Winton as well as designing for other companies.

In 1953 Bruce decided to move the company to 11654 McBean Dr., El Monte, California.

The Hillbilly Line was so popular that it forced the boys to build a 5000 square foot factory of their own at 1190 North Fair Oaks in Pasadena, California.

Along with the airbrushing and hand decorating, the woodtone finish was developed after Bruce bought the company and moved it to El Monte. Don started creating the winsome line of characters for the entire collection at that time. Cookie jars, salt & pepper sets, and related household accessories such as spoon rests, wall pockets, planters, kegs, napkin holders, and lamps are some of the items created. After moving the factory to El Monte, Bruce needed to hire some salesmen. He tried several including a jobber Wm. Hirsch. By 1961, according to Jay (Cook) Potter the bookkeeper for 25 years, Hirsch was only a memory. This places the Hirsch product between 1953 and 1960. It is important to note that Hirsch was not a manufacturer and that he bought products from several other ceramics companies. Not every Hirsch piece was designed by Don nor was it necessarily manufactured by Twin Winton.

Another salesman, Victor Bonomo, said he worked for Bruce from 1955 till Twin Winton closed. They only had 10 to 15 cookie jars in the line in 1955. They also had other products such as the dish

Figurines designed in Pasadena and El Monte.

lines, wall pockets, and decorator items. Victor said that the man that really made a difference for Twin Winton was Bill Wagner. Bill sold the entire line to J. C. Penney Company. Part of the deal for Penney's to carry the line was that a full catalog had to be developed. This means that catalogs were in existence from approximately 1954 until approximately 1975.

Three of the Twin Winton cookie jars from J. C. Penney Company catalog, Christmas 1972.

Bruce kept the business in El Monte until 1964 when he made the decision to move to San Juan Capistrano, California. Brad Keeler, another California pottery manufacturer, had died and his factory was for sale. Brad had someone create a mural outside his building that still stands today in San Juan Capistrano as an historical landmark. Today that mural is known as the mural that stood outside the Twin Winton Factory. Bruce kept the factory in San Juan Capistrano until 1976 when he sold it to Roger Bowermeister and sons. The Bowermeisters ran the business for a year trying different glazes but were unable to make enough money to support themselves. After only one year the Bowermeisters declared bankruptcy and the business went back to Bruce. He decided to auction off the assets including the molds. Al Levin of Treasure Craft bought the molds and produced some of the designs under the Treasure Craft name. These molds have since been destroyed, the year they were destroyed is unclear.

LEARNING IS FUN!—A group of Capistrano Unified students were treated to a change of pace in the summer schedule with field trips sponsored by the Parents Association for Gifted Education. Here Bruce Winton explains his firm's pottery process to those taking a tour of local industries, who opened their doors to the eager youngsters. Another field trip led by a geologist focused on area a﹍ heology. Other groups participated in an amateur radio class taught by Rip Frater of Niguel and a sailing course, arranged by PAGE. Nonnie Leeburd and Beverly DuPui﹍ of Niguel handled arrangements.

Bruce in the San Juan Capistrano factory.

Mural from outside the Twin Winton factory, now an historical monument.

Factory in San Juan Capistrano.

Ross was a master mold maker and great salesman. Don said Ross was the best mold maker he had ever seen. He was an adventurer and was always willing to try something new. After Ross and Don sold Twin Winton to Bruce, Ross sold architectural ornaments under the name "The Twin Winton Designers." He sold some wall ornaments to a bank in Texas, and then had Don design the 12 stations of the cross for Sacred Heart Episcopal Church of Covina, California. The Claremont Colleges commissioned Don and Ross to make their logo "The Sower." The dimensions of the piece were 2½' x 2½'. Anything Ross could sell, Don could design.

In 1971 Ross and Kirk (Ross's son) opened the Twinton Line. They decided to try a line designed by Don and manufactured in Japan. There were 20 designs of children along with the Twinton stand. These were sold at the J.C. Pen-

Ross and Don kneeling over an architectural ornament for a building.

ney stores throughout the nation. Ross and Kirk closed Twinton in 1976. In 1977 Ross discovered he had a brain tumor which he died from in March 1980. Upon Ross's death, the family discovered a lot of Twinton figures in the basement of his home. His sons wanted to get rid of these and tried everything they could think of to sell them. Finally Kirk and Cam decided to load up a flat bed truck and made two trips to the dump.

There were three trips that Ross and Joann (Ross's wife) made to Japan. When Ross went, Bruce decided to try reviving the Hillbilly Line and ordered certain pieces he thought would sell. Apparently this was not a big seller because Bruce could not sell the pieces and had to sell them at a discount to get some of his money back. On these same trips Ross also ordered several decanters made for Stetzel Weller Liquor. These included the Hillbilly on a Barrel, Rebel Yell, and others.

Workers inspecting the Hillbilly decanters.

Ross in Japan inspecting a decanter being made for Stetzel Weller.

Don was freelance sculpting from 1952 to the present day. He not only sculpted for his brothers, but many other ceramics, trophy, and toy companies. Below I have listed some of the companies that he has designed for since 1952. See if you recognize any of the names.

ACME Hardware	Hamm's Beer	U.S. Plastic
Enjoying Marriage	Smithsonian	Chevy Dealers
Rembrandt Pottery	Brad Keeler	McCullough Pottery
Agape Porcelain	Hanna Barbera	University California Irvine
Florence Ceramics	Snyder, Charlie	Chicken of the Sea
Republican Committee	Bradford Exchange	McFarlan Pottery
Alberta Ceramics	Hirsch & Co.	UCLA Hall of Fame
Franklin Mint	Starns, Walter	Chuck Missler
Revell Toys	Brayton Laguna Pottery	Merle Norman Cosmetics
American Bisque	Irvine Co.	United Way
Fresno-Hall of Fame	Sun Foundry	Coca-Cola
Rexall Drug	Brush Pottery	MJB
Amway	Johannes Brahm	University of Nevada
Frito Co.	Sun Rubber Co.	Colgate Co.
Rio Hondo Ceramics	Burgermeister	Nine Lives
Arrow Liquor	Kenner Toys	Van de Kamps
G.O.P. Women	Sylvan Ceramics	David Ben-Gurion University
Roberta Ceramics	Busch Gardens	Open Door Company
Arrow Rubber Co.	Kipp Ceramics	Victoria Station
Gabriel Porcelain	T-W Imports (Bruce)	DeForrest
Roerig, Joyce	California Plush Toys	Pan American Airlines
Artistic Awards	Kool Aid	Virginia Slims
General Electric	T.V. Academy	Democratic Committee
Rottweiler Dog Club	California Clock Co.	Partridge Stamp
Avnet Awards (Trophy fig.)	L.A. Times	Walker Potteries
General Foods (Mermaid)	Thomas Ceramics	Disneyland
Sacred Heart Episcopal Church	Calvary Chapel	Plastic Dress Up (Trophies)
Bacardi Rum	Laura Scudder	Witness Pottery
Gerber Toys	Times Mirror	Dodge
Scripto	Campus Crusade	Purex
Bass, Diane	Link Corp.	Woodland Ceramics
Gilner Pottery	Tonka-Vogue	Dove Porcelain
Servite High School	Carnation	Rainbow Plastics
Bell Helmets	Loraines Ceramics	Wright, Norma J.
Goode Imports	Treasure Craft (Al Levin)	Duncan Royale
Shalom International	Cemar Pottery	Reagan Foundation
Ben Hur (MGM)	Mattel Toy Co.	YMCA
Hagen-Renaker	Trojan Club	Elk Trophy Co.
Sierra Madre Ceramics	Ceramichrome	Reagan Library
Bob's Big Boy (Bank & CJ)	Max Factor	Zodiak Products

I was recently (May 1997) with Don and Norma at their house and Don was telling me about the creative process he goes through in designing a new sculpture. I was fortunate enough to have my camera and snapped a couple of pictures while he and Norma were talking. I simply call it the many faces of Don Winton.

"I have an idea!"

"Not quite right..."

"I need a new perspective, Norma!!"

"How's this!" said Norma. "Not exactly what I had in mind," replied Don.

May you have many more years of continued creativity and joy and we look forward to the designs that will bring future generations as much happiness as we have experienced.

VALUE CHARACTERISTICS

Any time you collect something, there are characteristics that make that collectible more or less valuable. I have listed below some of these characteristics in the hope that as you hunt for your treasures, you will have a guide on values.

Designer – Since our focus is on Don Winton, can you confirm he designed the piece you are considering? All of these were in reputable antique stores with tags identifying the manufacturer as Twin Winton. They all had characteristics and the look. None of these were in fact made by Don.

Marking – Can you read the original marking from the manufacturer. (Just because it has been tagged by the seller as Twin Winton does not mean it really was manufactured by them.) The mug was marked Twin Winton by a store tag but is definitely not made by him. The moon chip and dip bowl is marked Twin Winton on the bottom and is in fact his but I never would have guessed this one, had not a dealer pointed it out.

Original Design – Has the piece you are looking at been copied or imitated by another artist from the original design. This squirrel was bought in San Diego and looks like an early Winton. It is 8" tall and the decorations look similar to the early Winton animals. The piece is not signed, and when shown to Don, he said the squirrel was too skinny, the tail was all wrong, and it was definitely not made by him.

Decoration – How well did the artist who decorated the piece accomplish the goal? This is important when looking at the pieces whether it be from a commercial company or an artist doing it for themselves. This Mother Goose cookie jar is a great example of superb decorating. It is Don's design and the decorator spent a lot of time on this piece. The Russian is a good example of a poor decorating job.

Hand Signed – You can add 20% or more to the value if the artist has signed the piece. His signature authenticates it as his rather than there being a question as to its origin. I remembered seeing this garlic pot in an old sales flier, Don confirmed it and signed it, thus authenticating the piece as his design.

Dimensions – Does the size of the piece match up in size to the original piece made by the manufacturer. You can see the size difference between the two sets of shakers. The smaller ones were marked by a dealer as Winton, but are not Don's. An artist copied and modified the smaller pieces. This is especially important if you only want product made by Twin Winton. The copies will lose approximately 20% of their size when they are copied from a piece as opposed to being made from an original mold.

Quantity Produced – Quantity of pieces made for distribution will affect availability. The "Cookie Jar Collector" stand only has 100 pieces that were produced which therefore affects how many collectors can own one.

Date of Manufacture – The date it was manufactured will sometimes affect the value. If it is one of his very early pieces it may be more valuable simply because it has stood the test of time. These older pieces are from the 1940s and are more difficult to locate.

Place of Manufacture – Where was it manufactured? Was it made by the Twin Winton factory or was it jobbed out to another manufacturer? The Twinton line was made overseas but some samples were made here in the states.

Hand Painted – by Don Winton. These are rare and will be hard to find. The only way to verify this is in writing by Don. I found this cow at a garage sale for .25¢. It had been used as a planter because the lid and horn had been broken and thrown away. Don took the cow, repaired her horn, made a new lid, and repainted her for me.

Condition – What is the condition of the piece? Will it take a minor repair or major restoration to get it back to original condition? This castle has a broken lid but is still valuable because it is a rarer jar and will be worth restoring.

Limited Edition – How many and is it verifiable? The ibex is a beautiful and verifiable limited edition.

Stock Numbers – Stock numbers were sometimes used more than once. If two pieces have the same catalog number it could cause confusion. One of the pieces was discontinued, possibly because it did not sell well. At least this is true with Twin Winton. The wheelbarrow is a good example. It was in only one catalog in 1971 as TW-62. The same stock number also refers to Barrel in the previous catalogs 1964 – 1968. When speaking of pieces, it is important to use terminology that everyone understands, the stock numbers help.

Price – This is the hardest consideration. This book will give you a guide. The final consideration is how much will a buyer pay to a seller to own the piece offered. This little chipmunk had a small chip, and it sold for only $3.00 in an antique store in San Diego. To me as a collector, it was worth much more. It is an early piece that I did not have in my collection and I would have paid more than that even with the chip.

Crispness of Detail – As the molds were used, the detail got less and less distinct. Was care given to maintain the original detail? Note the bank has much more detail than the cookie jar around the face, the arms, and on the stomach. The bank was most likely one of the first ones out of the mold and the jar was probably one from the middle of the run.

Name –Name of the piece is extremely important. I will refer to the pieces in this book by the name given in the catalog or sales flier, where possible. If not available, I will use the common popular name. Sailor Elephant is the popular name; in the catalog it is known simply as Elephant.

One of a Kind Originals – This can only be identified by the artist himself with a letter or certificate by him. Don has records from 1952 through the present in which he has written down every piece he has made and for whom he made it. The "Don and Norma Jar" in the last chapter is a good example of a one of a kind original.

Each of these items will affect the value of your piece and should be considered when making the purchase. I feel that just because a piece has a flaw it should not be overlooked. If I demanded mint condition perfect pieces before I bought anything I would have lost the joy of my collecting a long time ago. After all, a little wear and tear on any item creates a mystery and history about the item.

MARKINGS

The markings, packaging, and product cards on the pieces created by Don Winton are as varied as his designs. The methods of marking include slip painting, permanent marker, ceramic stamp, incising into the mold (bottom or side), stamp under glaze, or gold seal decal. The imprint used can be Winton, Twin Winton, B-W, Burke-Winton, TW-#, Twin Winton Designs, Twin Winton-Pasadena, Twin Winton-El Monte, Twin Winton-San Juan Capistrano, Open Range Line, Mountaineer Line, Ladies of the Mountain, Bronco Group, Bamboo Line, Agape Porcelain, Shekinah China, Twinton, or any number of others yet to be identified. This list does not include any of the markings on Don's designs from other companies like Treasure Craft, Brush, Florence Ceramics, Ideas Inc., Merle Norman, Sun Rubber Toy Co., Alberta Molds, etc. I have simply listed, below the pictures, a category for ease of identification and a time period.

Other companies have a variety of markings and research will have to continue to show more at a later date.

Packaging for the wood finish cookie jar shipped from San Juan Capistrano. Value: $30.00.

Packaging for the collector finish cookie jar shipped from San Juan Capistrano. Value: $40.00.

Gold seal label used in later years — approximately mid 1970s. Also used by Bowermeisters.

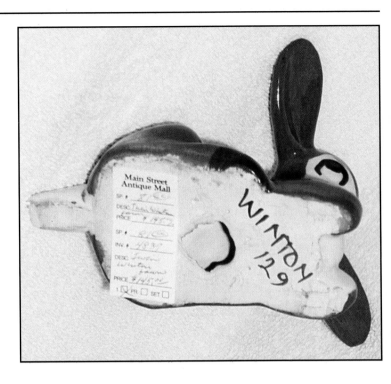

Early animals and figures were marked by a simple identification on the bottom. Used from 1936 to 1941.

This incised and stained marking on the bear bud vase was used from 1950 to 1952.

Artist palette on the bottom of a line of dishes used from 1950 to 1952.

Twinton stamp was only used on the imported children figurines in 1972.

Ceramic stamp found on early items dated 1946 to 1952. This dating has been verified by Don's signature in this photo.

Hand written on the bottom of a pitcher owned by Don's sister-in-law. Dated 1946 – 1952.

Under glaze hand-written ink found on a pair of early salt and pepper shakers. Dated 1947 – 1950.

Open Range line and brand on the bottom of this mug from the Bronco Group. 1951 – 1952

Incised on the bottom of a Hillbilly punch bowl. Note the date March 30, 1949.

Incised on the bottom of a Hillbilly mug.

Incised on a Hillbilly ashtray from the Mountaineer line, 1947 – 1950.

Incised on a mug from the Bronco group being developed in March 1949.

In the mold on the bottom of a decanter it reads "A Twin Winton Design Pasadena, CA An Oriental Import." Some of the decanters read this way, some read Alberta Molds, and some have only a number.

Under glaze on a mug from the Bamboo Line of dishes, 1950 – 1952.

Incised on the bottom of a foo dog salt shaker.

Under the paint and glaze on a Volkswagen bank. It reads "Twin Winton San Juan Capistrano," 1964 – 1974.

Incised on the bottom of a tumbler from The Bar Brand Line, 1950 – 1952.

Incised on the bottom of a chip n dip bowl. It reads "Twin Winton USA."

Hand written by Don Winton in 1996 to verify the manufacture date in 1947. This is on the bottom of the early Hillbilly pour spout display.

BURKE WINTON

BURKE WINTON

Two markings used on early pieces while working with Helen Burke, 1937. (They also used the letter BW and a number.)

The ceramic stamp has two versions. Both say Twin Winton. One says "California USA" and the other says "San Juan Capistrano, Calif. USA."

Found on the bottom of a piece made by Don for sale in 1974.

Incised on the bottom of a bamboo looking planter. I was surprised when I found this piece but Don says he made some of these for special requests. Mid 1970s.

Incised on the bottom of a Barrel cookie jar. Note the marking above the Twin Winton name. It is believed that these were marked for William Hirsch although it is unconfirmed. Hirsch was a jobber and wanted his name very prominent on the pieces he sold. (I believe it could be the initials of either the caster or the decorator.)

ORIGINAL ARTWORK

Ever wonder what an artist is thinking?

The creative process is one that is ever growing and changing. Don Winton in his creative genius is no different. The drawings shown in this chapter are part of the growth that Don goes through in the creation of his designs and original artwork. The final design in ceramic, porcelain, bronze, or other media more often than not is different from the sketch that he has drawn. However, when he initially starts giving birth to these pieces of art that give us so much pleasure he starts with a sketch. These pencil sketches carefully drawn on delicate tissue paper or regular notebook paper are ideas directly from the mind of Don. When initially discovering some of these, they were stuffed in file folders, boxes in the garage, and miscellaneous drawers in his studio. Norma has told Don on more than one occasion that he should get rid of some of the junk in their house. I asked him and Norma if they realized the value of these wonderful drawings. Norma mentioned that Diane Bass, a friend, had said the art was valuable and she and Don were thinking that they should start taking better care of them. The question was answered when one was sold at auction for $700.00. These one-of-a-kind drawings are currently valued from $500.00 – 2,000.00. These wonderful designs are now being carefully preserved. Some of them will be sold in the near future through the Twin Winton Collector Club, dealers, and auctions throughout the country. In preparing these for this book I absolutely fell in love with some of these wonderful drawings and I hope you enjoy them.

Frog & Dog Toothbrush Holder – 9" x 12"

Kristy Kangaroo Bottle Holder – 8½" x 11"   Skunk Air Wick Bottle – 8½" x 11"

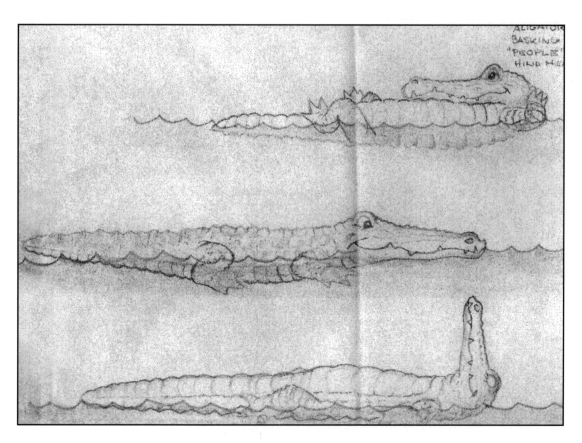

Three Alligator Floating Toys – 11" x 14"

Cinderella's Pumpkin Coach – 9" x 12"

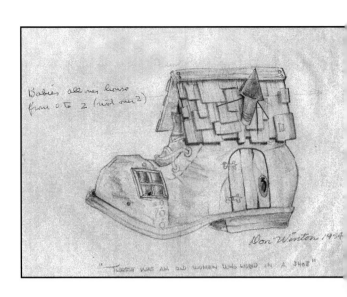

There Was an Old Woman who Lived in a Shoe
8½" x 11"

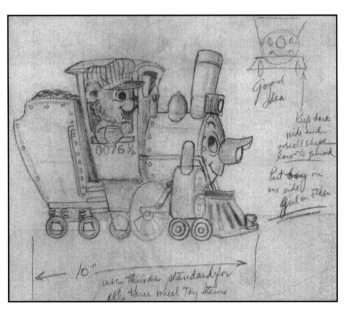

Train Wheel Toy – 11" x 14"

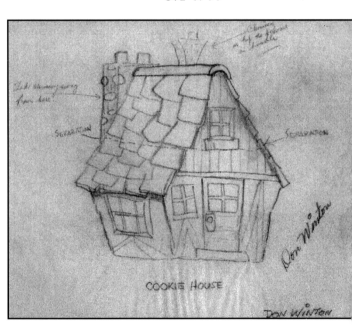

Cookie House – 9" x 12"

Four Penquin Pull Toy – 9" x 12"

Bear in Honey Pot – 9" x 12"

Squirrel with Nut and Mallet – 9" x 12"

Happy Bunny – 9" x 12"

Racoon Cookie Jar – 9" x 12"

Three Smiling Cats – 9" x 12"

Pig Eating Cookie and Dog in Basket – 9" x 12"

Panda, Chick, Clown Duck,
Sitting Puppy, and Pup in Shoe – 11" x 14"

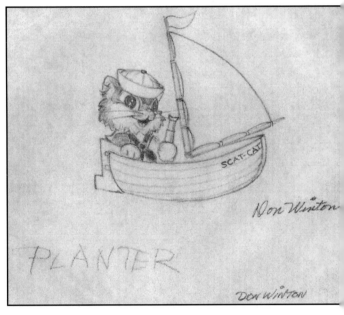

Cat in Salboat Planter – 8½" x 11"

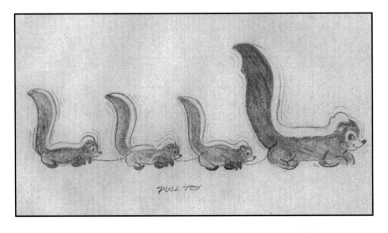

Four Skunk Pull Toy – 8½" x 11"

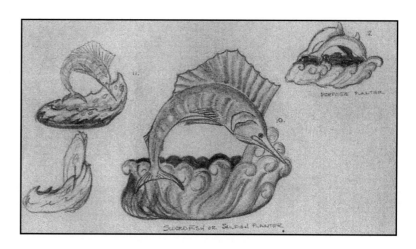

Two Fish Planters – 8½" x 11"   Sword Fish or Snail Fish Planter – 8½" x 11"

Rooster Lamp – 8½" x 11"

Gazelle Ashtray – 8½" x 11"

ALBERTA'S MOLDS, INC.

In my research for this book I kept coming across the name Alberta's Molds, Inc. I learned that Alberta Gaskell was still alive and well and living in California. I called and explained that I was doing a book on Don Winton designs and she sent me the following letter.

"We became acquainted with the Winton brothers, Bruce, Ross, and Don in the early 1950s when we purchased some of their discontinued designs. One of the first pieces we purchased was our #100 fishing boy which later became our logo. We then purchased some little baseball and football players. The pieces had so much detail that it was not suitable for commercial purposes since it required so much decorating but was just the thing for ceramic hobbyists. Don was the artist and the one who did the modeling. We persuaded him to do some models for us which he did for the next 30 years. We liked his sense of whimsy. We never knew what surprise we would find when we received our models, such as a small raccoon peeking out from behind a branch or a mouse perched atop a log. He was very versatile and modeled delicate figurines and natural looking animals as well as whimsical pieces. He did all his modeling with the help of a very small pen knife and I never saw him use any other modeling tool."

Signed,
Alberta Gaskell
Alberta's Molds, Inc.

In looking through a 1980 catalog of Alberta's Molds, I came across this wonderful article on "The Making of a Mold." Since Don designed the "Small Snow White" on the following page, I felt it would be of interest to let you see the process. Sometimes we forget how much work is involved in getting a single piece from the idea stage through to the final decorated piece.

Catalog sheet of "The Making Of A Mold"

Established in 1949, Alberta started purchasing Don's designs about a year after she started her company. This is fortunate for Don because this coincides with the decline of the popularity of the Hillbilly line by Twin Winton. It is also necessary to note that Alberta purchased some of the molds from Twin Winton that did not sell well for some reason. That is why you may see Twin Winton incised on the bottom of a piece and you may find the same design with Alberta's Molds on the bottom. The people who have purchased Alberta's molds have a love of art and are artists in their own rights. Some of the decorating that I have seen has been absolutely magnificent and some looks terrible. The value on these pieces are based upon the characteristics listed in the chapter "Value Characteristics." These values are for mint condition, carefully decorated items. I have some of these in my collection and find them delightful.

CHRISTMAS ORNAMENTS

SYMBOL OF QUALITY

#A-121

#A-122

#A-123

#A-124

#A-125

#A-126

All Alberta's Christmas ornaments have designs on both sides

Each Ornament Approximately 3-5/8" high or long — 9.2 cm

#A-127

#A-128

These whimsical Christmas ornaments have designs on both sides and are approximately 3⅝" high or long. The values on these items range from $3.00 to $8.00 depending on difficulty of casting and decorating.

A-121 – $6.00, A-122 – $4.00, A-123 – $4.00, A-124 – $4.00,
A-125 – $5.00, A-126 – $8.00, A-127 – $6.00, A-128 – $5.00.

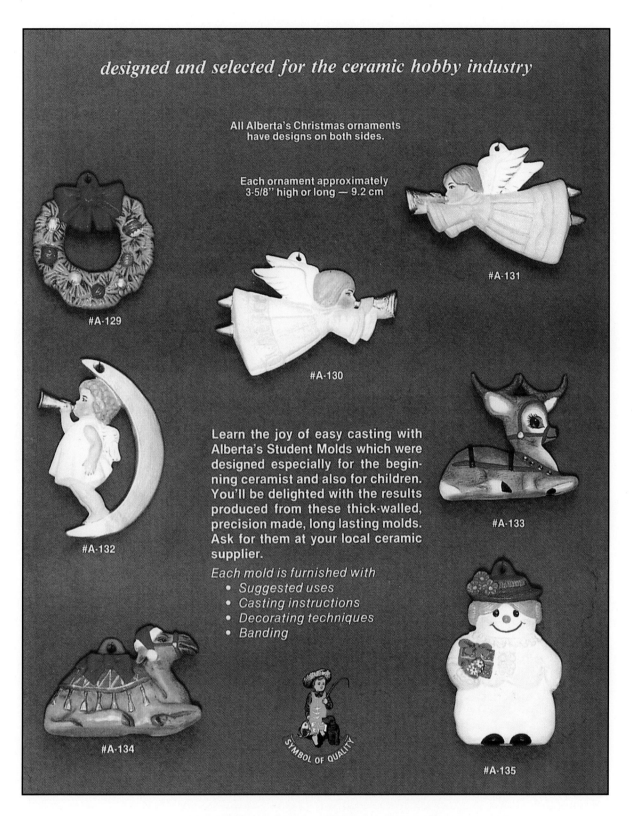

designed and selected for the ceramic hobby industry

All Alberta's Christmas ornaments have designs on both sides.

Each ornament approximately 3-5/8" high or long — 9.2 cm

#A-129

#A-130

#A-131

#A-132

Learn the joy of easy casting with Alberta's Student Molds which were designed especially for the beginning ceramist and also for children. You'll be delighted with the results produced from these thick-walled, precision made, long lasting molds. Ask for them at your local ceramic supplier.

Each mold is furnished with
- *Suggested uses*
- *Casting instructions*
- *Decorating techniques*
- *Banding*

#A-133

#A-134

SYMBOL OF QUALITY

#A-135

A-129 – $5.00, A-130 – $4.00, A-131 – $4.00,
A-132 – $8.00, A-133 – $6.00, A-134 – $6.00, A-135 – $6.00.

A-53, $6.00, A-54 – $8.00, A-56 – $6.00.

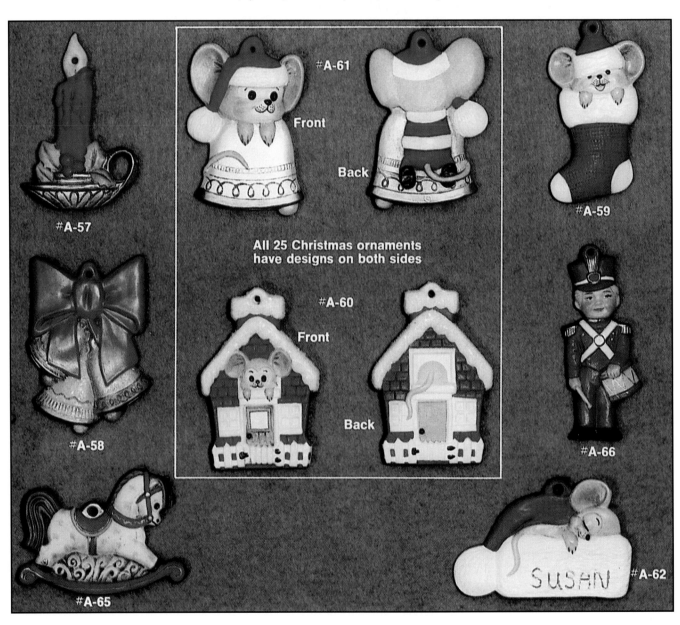

A-57 – $6.00, A-58 – $5.00, A-59 – $6.00, A-60 – $8.00,
A-61 – $8.00, A-62 – $4.00, A-65 – $6.00, A-66 – $6.00.

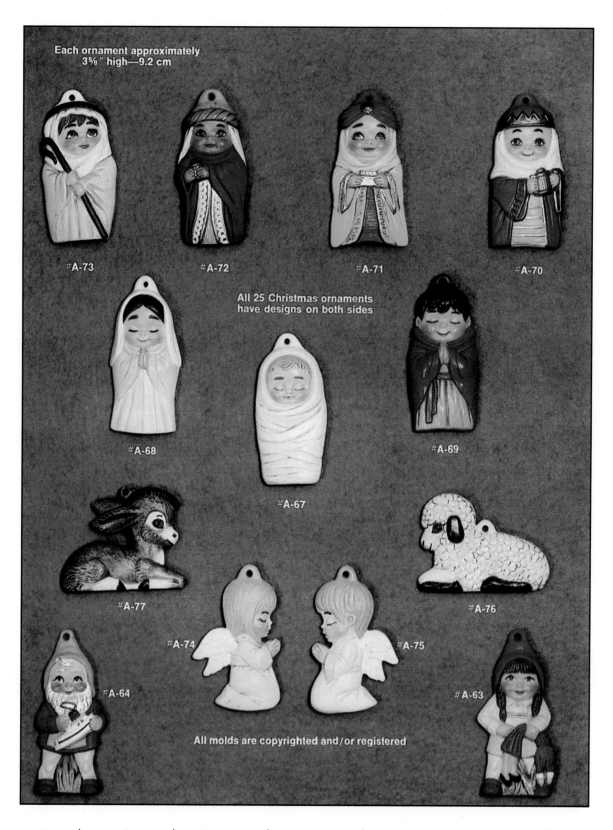

Each ornament approximately
3⅝" high—9.2 cm

#A-73   #A-72   #A-71   #A-70

All 25 Christmas ornaments
have designs on both sides

#A-68   #A-67   #A-69

#A-77   #A-74   #A-75   #A-76

#A-64   #A-63

All molds are copyrighted and/or registered

A-73 – $5.00, A-72 – $5.00, A-71 – $5.00, A-68 – $5.00, A-67 – $5.00, A-69 – $5.00,
A-77 – $6.00, A-74 – $6.00, A-75 – $6.00, A-76 – $4.00, A-64 – $8.00, A-63 – $8.00.

Don's love of the child-like elves is well known to any that have gotten to know his work. These ageless little elves will continue to bring joy and the remembrance of childhood fantasies and dreams to all who see them.

A-36 FLOWER POT GNOME WITH WATERING CAN
5⅛" high - 13 cm. high. 5 pounds, 2.3 kilograms

A-39 FLOWER POT SLEEPING GNOME
3-5/16" high - 8.4 cm. high. 3 pounds, 1.4 kilograms

A-40 FLOWER POT SITTING GNOME *
5-7/16" high - 13.9 cm. high. 5 pounds, 2.3 kilograms
*Shown on #562 Bench

A-41 FLOWER POT GNOME WITH WHEELBARROW
5⅛" high - 13 cm. high. 5 pounds, 2.3 kilograms

A-36 – $8.00, A-39 – $8.00, A-40 – $12.00, A-41 – $10.00.

A-42 FLOWER POT GNOME ON LADDER
5½" high - 14 cm. high. 8 pounds,
3.6 kilograms

A-44 FLOWER POT GIRL GNOME
5-3/16" high - 13.2 cm. high. 4 pounds,
1.8 kilograms

A-52 SMALL SNOW WHITE
7⅛" high - 18.1 cm. high. 7 pounds,
3.2 kilograms

A-37 FLOWER POT GNOME WITH CLIPPERS
4¾" high - 12.1 cm. high. 5 pounds, 2.3 kilograms

A-38 FLOWER POT GNOME WITH SHOVEL
5-3/16" high - 13.2 cm. high. 5 pounds, 2.3 kilograms

A-42 – $8.00, A-44 – $12.00, A-37 – $8.00, A-38 – $8.00, A-52 – $12.00.

#544 RECLINING GNOME   12½" long — 45 lbs.
#545 STANDING GNOME   12½" high — 30 lbs.
#546 SITTING GNOME*   10½" high — 34 lbs.
#587 SEATED GNOME   8" high — 18 lbs.
#588 SNOOZIN' GNOME   4" high 9" long — 24 lbs.
#589 NAPPING GNOME   6" high 9" long — 30 lbs.
#590 KNEELING GNOME   7" high 10" long — 46 lbs.
#603 SNOW WHITE ●● 20¾" high — 23+101 lbs.
*Seated on bottom of #478 Jam Jar

#544 – $20.00, #587 – $20.00, #590 – $20.00, #589 – $20.00,
#588 – $20.00, #545 – $20.00, #546 – $20.00, #603 – $50.00.

The small figures of children playing pictured in the following illustrations give you an insight into the way Don sees kids. Similar figures also show up with a Twin Winton stamp on the bottom. They were initially designed as part of a line for distribution for the Twin Winton factory, but because of the amount of detailing and time it took to manufacture the pieces, they were sold to Alberta for the home hobbyist. Please note that the value listed for these are based on the Alberta name being incised on the bottom. The Twin Winton factory stamp increases the value as listed in the Twin Winton figures section of this book.

Great Performers

A-35 HOCKEY PLAYER
5½" high - 14 cm. high. 5 pounds, 2.3 kilograms

A-470 BALLERINA
3¾" high - 9.5 cm. high. 3 pounds, 1.4 kilograms

A-50 SOCCER PLAYER
5¼" high - 13.3 cm. high. 5 pounds, 2.3 kilograms

A-568 BASEBALL PITCHER
5½" high - 13 cm. high. 5 pounds, 2.3 kilograms

A-569 BASEBALL BATTER
5½" high - 13 cm. high. 5 pounds, 2.3 kilograms

A-570 BASEBALL CATCHER
4¼" high - 10.8 cm. high. 5 pounds, 2.3 kilograms

A-571 BASEBALL UMPIRE
5" high - 12.7 cm. high. 5 pounds, 2.3 kilograms

A-49 BASKETBALL PLAYER
5¾" high - 14.6 cm. high. 5 pounds, 2.3 kilograms

A-573 FOOTBALL PLAYER
5½" high - 13 cm. high. 5 pounds, 2.3 kilograms

A-572 FOOTBALL PLAYER
5½" high - 13 cm. high. 5 pounds, 2.3 kilograms

A-48 CHEERLEADER
5½" high - 14 cm. high. 5 pounds, 2.3 kilograms

A-35 – $15.00, A-470 – $12.00, A-50 – $15.00, A568 – $15.00, A-569 – $15.00, A-570 – $15.00, A-571 – $15.00, A-49 – $15.00, A-573 – $15.00, A-572 – $15.00, A-48 – $15.00.

#658 set – $100.00.

#722 – $ 50.00.

#610 – $30.00, #611 – $25.00, #612 – $25.00, #636 – $40.00,
#637 – $25.00, #638 – $35.00, #639 – $15.00.

Kittens have always caught Don's attention because of their curiosity and expressiveness. In looking at these wonderful creations I almost expect them to start talking.

A-180, $8.00.

A-84 Set – $10.00.

A-178 KITTEN "GUSSIE"
¼" high - 5.7 cm. high. 3 pounds, 1.4 kilograms

A-179 KITTEN "MUFFY"
2¼" high - 5.7 cm. high. 3 pounds, 1.4 kilograms

A-178 – $8.00, A-179 – $10.00.

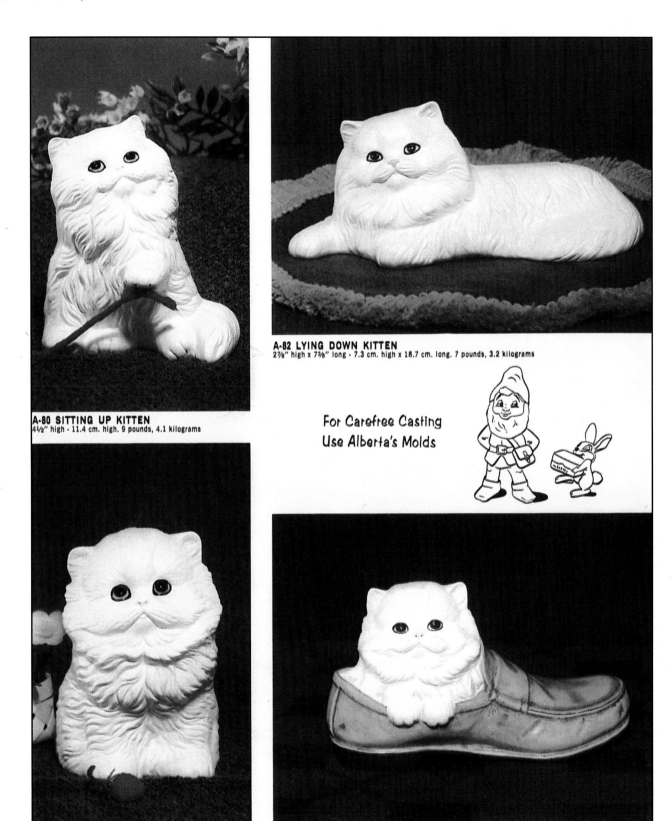

A-80 SITTING UP KITTEN
4½" high · 11.4 cm. high. 9 pounds, 4.1 kilograms

A-82 LYING DOWN KITTEN
2⅞" high x 7⅜" long · 7.3 cm. high x 18.7 cm. long. 7 pounds, 3.2 kilograms

For Carefree Casting
Use Alberta's Molds

A-81 SITTING KITTEN
4½" high · 11.4 cm. high. 9 pounds, 4.1 kilograms

A-83 KITTEN IN SHOE
3⅞" high x 6¾" long · 9.8 cm. high x 17.2 cm. long. 7 pounds, 3.2 kilograms

A-80 – $12.00, A-82 – $15.00, A-81 – $12.00, A-83 – $15.00.

From the whimsical to the rugged, Don has the ability to make the transition. These figures are not mild and meek, but men of action, ready to handle any situation whether it be in the mountains, on the plains, or in the Middle Ages.

MOUNTAIN MAN W/HAT •• 18½" high	INDIAN W/SHIELD & QUIVER •• 17¾" high	COWBOY W/HAT •• 18¾" high
#760 MOUNTAIN MAN—88 lbs.	#759 INDIAN—74 lbs.	#758 COWBOY—89 lbs.
#760A HAT—8½ lbs.	#759A SHIELD & QUIVER—12 lbs.	#758A HAT—6 lbs.

#760 – $85.00, #759 – $100.00, #758 – $75.00.

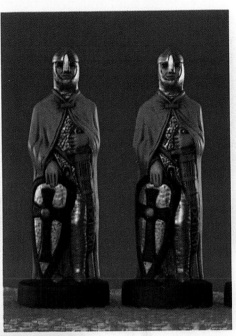

Chess Set

A-13-A KING/QUEEN CHESS SET
King: 5⅞" high - 15 cm. high; Queen: 5½" high - 14 cm. high, 6 pounds, 2.7 kilograms

A-13-B BISHOP/KNIGHT/CASTLE CHESS SET
Bishop: 5¼" high - 13.3 cm. high; Knight: 4¾" high - 12.1 cm. high; Castle: 4⅝" high - 11.8 cm. high, 6 pounds, 2.7 kilograms

A-13-C PAWNS CHESS SET
4-7/16" high - 11.3 cm. high, 6 pounds, 2.7 kilograms
This mold produces 4 pawns.

A-13 King – $12.00, A-13-A Queen – $10.00, A-13-B Bishop – $10.00,
A-13-B Knight – $18.00, A-A-13-C Pawns – $7.00.

There is much more Don has created for Alberta's Molds. Also many riddles of Twin Winton are being solved through the study of the old molds that were bought by Alberta. You will find more of the Alberta's Molds products in other parts of the book listed by item.

DECANTERS

The many decanters that Don created again show the gift of creativity and variety that this man has shared with us all. Although decanters have recently gone down in value the standard for pricing is still the MONTAGUE'S PRICE GUIDE FOR DECANTERS (now out of print).

One notable piece that is currently being collected is the Kentucky Hillbilly. It was designed by Don Winton for Stitzel Weller Distillery in 1968. The earliest version has three sizes and was not designed by Don, nor did he design any of the pieces that look similar to the 1954 version. I found a label on the one Don designed in a store in Pasadena and felt you would enjoy the story.

1954 decanter (not Don's)
11⅜" x 4¼", $25.00.
Bottom reads: "D-379 139 Federal Law Forbids Sale Or Re-Use Of This Bottle."
This one comes in three sizes.

1968 decanter created by Don
11¼" x 4", $30.00.
(This is the only size for this decanter.)

Bottom of 1968 decanter.
Don's signature is not normally on the bottom.
If he has signed the piece add 20% to the value.

Collectors of fine porcelains, ceramics and figurines will prize this hand-crafted decanter which portrays the legendary Kentucky Hillbilly with great whimsey and artistic detail.

Produced as a limited edition, this is the second of a series of fanciful characters from the Kentucky bluegrass where great Bourbon was born. The first Hillbilly figurine, produced in 1954, is now in the hands of a small group of collectors throughout this country and has greatly enhanced in value through the years. Undoubtedly, this 1968 companion subject will be as eagerly sought after because it is beautifully executed and in limited supply.

This Kentucky Hillbilly contains a fifth of premium quality Cabin Still Kentucky straight Bourbon whiskey which is fully aged in deep-charred white mountain oak. The whiskey is identical to the Cabin Still Bourbon in your conventional bottle which is nationally famous as . . .

"The Sportsman's Bourbon."

As with the figurine, expert craftsmanship has gone into the creation of this genuine sour mash Bourbon. When this delightful Bourbon is consumed, you will still have an attractive collector's item which will increase in value with the years.

Hang tag on 1968 decanter, $15.00.

Old Hickory is one that is in a lot of antique stores. I heard Don had created many decanters and had seen one or two of them. I ran across this one and took it to Don and asked him if he by chance designed this. He smiled and said, "Oh yes! Would you like to see the original wax!" He went to his studio and pulled out the wax figure he had saved all of these years. Norma said, "I thought I told you to throw that out years ago!" Don grinned sheepishly as I explained that this piece is worth a lot of money. Norma then said, "I guess I shouldn't make him throw all this stuff out then."

Old Hickory decanter
11¼" x 3¼", $25.00.
Bottom reads "Old Hickory Distilling
Corporation."

Original wax of Old Hickory
14" x 4", too rare to value.
Only one in existence.

The Robin Hood decanter, I have to admit, is somewhat of a mystery. I found decanter number one in San Juan Capistrano at a local antique store. The second one pictured, I found at a friend's house in San Diego. The third I found in a store in Pasadena. The first one is a sample created for approval by the Pasadena Twin Winton factory for Arrow Liquor. The second one was made by Twin Winton but the terminology on the bottom for what the decanter was made from was incorrect and the government would not allow them to continue manufacture of the product. The third one was the one that was actually manufactured by Gabriel Ceramics for distribution.

Robin Hood decanter
11½" x 3⅞", $500.00.
Marking on bottom reads
"A Twin Winton Design -
Pasadena, Ca."
Only 6 to 12 of this one were
made.

Robin Hood decanter
10½" x 4⅜", $100.00.
Manufactured and distributed by
Twin Winton for Arrow.
Marking on bottom reads
"Hand-crafted Porcelain by Winton-
Pasadena."

Robin Hood decanter
10½" x 4⅜", $40.00.
Manufactured by Gabriel Pottery
for Arrow.
Marking on bottom reads
"Hand Crafted China By Gabriel
Of Pasadena."

The decanters listed below were designed by Don Winton in the early 1950s. Some of these were bought by Alberta Molds and Ceramichrome, Inc. The markings (shown in parenthesis next to the prices) could be one of four:

      A. "A Twin Winton Design - Pasadena, Ca"
      B. "Hand-crafted Porcelain by Winton-Pasadena"
      C. "Alberta Molds"
      D. "Ceramichrome, Inc."

For purposes of value, I have listed them by what most likely is on the bottom. Bottoms that read "A Twin Winton Design - Pasadena, Ca" appear to be samples that were prepared for presentation for possible manufacture. Keep your eyes open for these, there should only be 6 to 12 of each of these. They may have been produced in larger quantities with a different etching on the bottom. If you locate these please let me know.

Bartender
10" x 4", $500.00 (A).
10" x 4", $100.00 (B).

Pink Elephants
11" x 4", $500.00 (A).
11" x 4", $100.00 (B).

Christmas Cheer (Santa)
10½" x 4", $500.00 (A).
10½" x 4", $100.00 (B).

Marking "C" or "D" listed later in this chapter.

Russian Cossack with Bomb
10½" x 4", $500.00 (A).
10½" x 4", $100.00 (B).

Frenchman
10¼" x 4", $500.00 (A).
12" x 4", $100.00 (B).
Southern Colonel
11" x 4", $500.00 (A).
11" x 4", $100.00 (B).

Robin Hood
11" x 4", $500.00 (A).
11" x 4", $100.00 (B).
Mark Twain
12½" x 4", $500.00 (A).
12½" x 4", $100.00 (B).

Russian
12" x 4", $500.00 (A).
12" x 4", $100.00 (B).
Monk Wax - too rare to value.

Monk
12" x 4", $500.00 (A).
12" x 4", $100.00 (B).

Matador
11½" x 4", $500.00 (A).
11½" x 4", $100.00 (B).

Cowboy
13" x 4", $500.00 (A).
13" x 4", $100.00 (B).

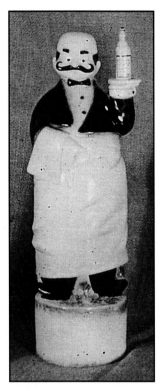

Waiter
11" x 4", $ 500.00 (A).
11" x 4", $ 100.00 (B).

Scotsman
11½" x 4", $500.00 (A).
11½" x 4", $100.00 (B).

Hillbilly
11" x 4", $500.00 (A).
11" x 4", $100.00 (B).

Indian
12½" x 4", $500.00 (A).
12½" x 4", $100.00 (B).

Fat Matador
11" x 4", $500.00 (A
11" x 4", $100.00 (B

The following two pages of decanters appeared in the 1980 catalog of Alberta Molds for the home-craft artists. The decorating definitely affects the price. These values are based on a quality decorating job similar to the ones pictured in the catalog. The bottom will most likely have "Alberta" incised on them. Some of these decanters were sold also by Ceramichrome, Inc. Therefore, they may have the name "Ceramichrome" on the bottom.

#615 – $50.00, #616 – $30.00, #617 – $75.00, #646 – #75.00, #647 – $30.00, #648 – $40.00, #659 – $40.00, #660 – #30.00, #661 – $75.00, #735 – $40.00, #736 – $30.00, #737 – #30.00.

#429 – $75.00, #430 – $40.00, #431 – $30.00, #432 – $50.00,
#433 – $30.00, #466 – $50.00, #498 – $75.00, #510 – $40.00,
#553 – $50.00, #554 – $40.00, #591 – $30.00, #592 – $40.00.

There are more decanters yet to be discovered and certainly more information to be revealed as we continue to investigate.

TROPHIES and BUSTS

Twin Winton was famous for many things throughout the years. One of the lesser known products was the trophies created. These as well are starting to become collectibles because of their unique construction.

This photo shows ceramic trophies with china gold paint made in 1950. They were created for the Gymnastic Championship in Pasadena. Sponsored by the Meguiar Bros. there were eight small ones and two large ones. The size is reported to be 12" for the small ones and 15" for the large ones.

12" Trophy – $75.00, 15" Trophy – $125.00.

This archival of the Apollo Award was created for the Chamber of Commerce in Fresno, California.

Model B-200G,

Model B-100,

Model B-200W,

Model B-500,

Golden Victory Trophies

by
Twin Winton
Pasadena, Calif.

Model B-400,

Model B-425,

Model B-450,

**Genuine Gold Finish
Won't Tarnish**

Top row, left to right:
Model B-200G, 8¼ ins. high
Model B-100, 7½ ins. high
Model B-200W, 8¼ ins. high
Model B-500, 9½ ins. high

Center row, left to right:
(Simulated Marble or Gold Base)
Model B-450, 16¾ ins. high
Model B-425, 14 ins. high
Model B-400, 11 ins. high

Bottom row, left to right:
(Simulated Marble or Gold Base)
Model B-300, 11 ins. high
Model B-325, 14 ins. high
Model B-350, 16¾ ins. high

Model B-300,

Model B-325,

Model B-350,

Golden Victory Trophies were ceramic trophies with china gold paint and were sold in the early to mid 1950s. You can see the sizes listed on this sales flier. The values will vary from $25.00 to $150.00.

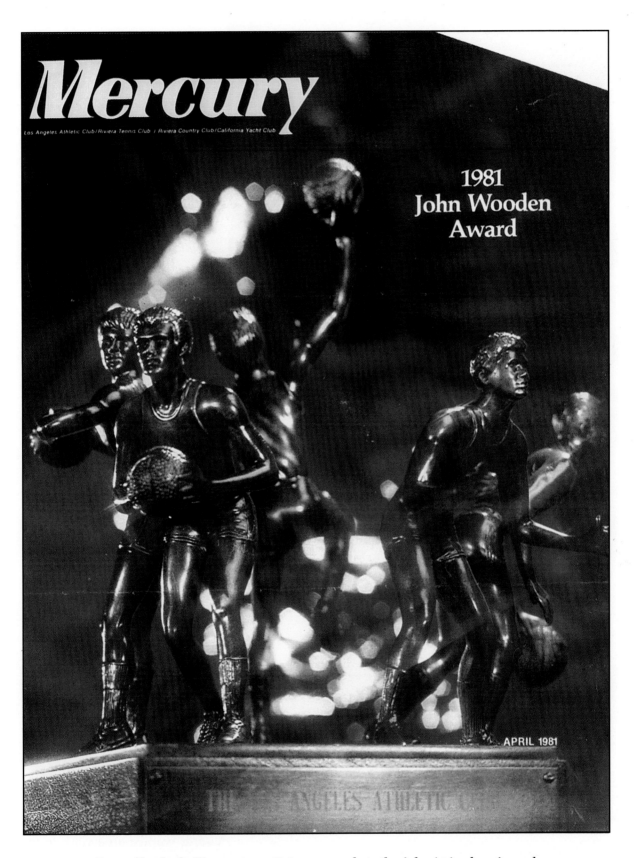

Mercury

Los Angeles Athletic Club/Riviera Tennis Club / Riviera Country Club/California Yacht Club

1981
John Wooden
Award

APRIL 1981

THE LOS ANGELES ATHLETIC CLUB

One of basketball's most prestigious awards is the John Wooden Award.
The figures were created by Don and are still used today.

Archival photo of the Fred Walton Memorial Trophy for the National AAU Pentathlon. This trophy was made of ceramic with the figure in china gold paint. It stood approximately 24". Value: $125.00.

Don puts the finishing touches on the model of a Russian family. This piece was eventually translated to a 15' statue set in front of Magic Mountain.

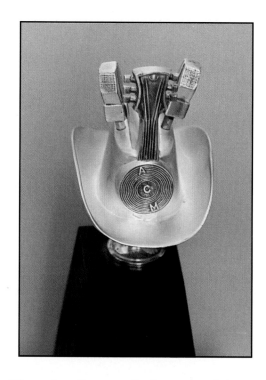

The Academy of Country Music Awards wanted an award to recognize their most famous personalities. This award is still being used today.

TVRegister

ᶜ ORANGE COUNTY'S TELEV... FOR THE WEEK OF MAY 7, 1995

CLINT BLACK AND TANYA TUCKER HOST THE 30TH ANNUAL ACADEMY OF COUNTRY MUSIC AWARDS ON NBC

Don designed the award pictured here (and on the previous page) for the Academy of Country Music Awards with Clint Black and Tanya Tucker hosting this prestigious event.

BUSINESS   Thursday, May 8, 1980   DAILY PILOT **B7**

Toy Sculpturing Real Work

LOS ANGELES (AP) — Most people associate sculptors with classic works displayed in museums. But Don Winton has carved a successful career with the Mickey Mouse telephone, the Grammy award and tub toys.

Winton, a soft-spoken 60-year-old, is a commercial sculptor whose other creations include the redesigned Emmy award, Disney and Hanna-Barbera toys and the Snoopy telephone. He has pursued his unique career for 32 years.

"GENERALLY, I'M commissioned by companies to create a character or other model which they can use for commercial purposes," says Winton. "I've also done aesthetic sculpturing, but my bread and butter is in the commercial field."

Winton often works from sketches or renderings but occasionally will develop his sculptures from scratch, as he did with the Laurel Wreath awards which Big Boy Restaurants and the American Heart Association commissioned to present to top American athletes.

"They've been a real challenge because there were no sketches to work from and the designs have to be stylized," said Winton. "The awards symbolize good health and physical fitness, so I've streamlined the sculpted figures and have them holding aloft the laurel wreath which dates back to the ancient Grecian games."

Winton has to work under other constraints. The Mickey Mouse telephone commissioned by General Telephone had to be sculpted so that the phone mechanism would fit in the base and arm. His toy sculptures are done with an eye to later mass production in rubber or vinyl and his trophy creations must be streamlined so they can be stamped out by machines.

Winton approaches his profession as a businessman, demanding cash in advance before he undertakes a project and following a strict schedule. However he occasionally works on speculation, as he did in 1947 when he offered to sculpt the Tournament of Roses queen who is now his wife.

"I had a real devious plan the whole way. I spotted her picture in the paper and I really felt a nudge," says Winton, who talked tournament officials into commissioning a sculpture. "I remember going to her home with my clay. She was beautiful, intelligent, and a year later we were married."

WINTON'S FEES RANGE from $1,500 to $25,000 — higher than they used to be.

"A few years ago, I began to realize that there's nobody else around doing commercial sculpturing and that I could raise my rates without losing customers," he said. "Now I just take the jobs I want to do."

Winton thinks the trophy and award field offers real opportunities for art students and has his eye on one trophy he thinks he could improve.

"I'd love to change that Heisman award," he says. "Of course that's tradition, and if yo changed it, eve   scream."

DON WINTON CARVES SUCCESSFUL CAREER
His Characters Pay Off Commercially

AP Wirephoto

The Virginia Slims Tennis Tournament is one that attracts top athletes from around the world. They all come for the prestige, money, and competition of playing a sport they love to earn a trophy designed by Don Winton. This article from the DAILY PILOT in May 1980 not only shows this award but it also shows the Laurel Wreath Award commissioned by Bob's Big Boy Restaurants and the American Heart Association. The article also mentions that Don created the Grammy Award.

This ceramic medallion was created for the decathlon competition at John Muir High School.
3", $25.00.

This coin was created for the movie BEN HUR. The movie company needed a coin that resembled a currency of ancient Rome and called upon Don.
2½" diameter, $75.00.

Back of medallion.

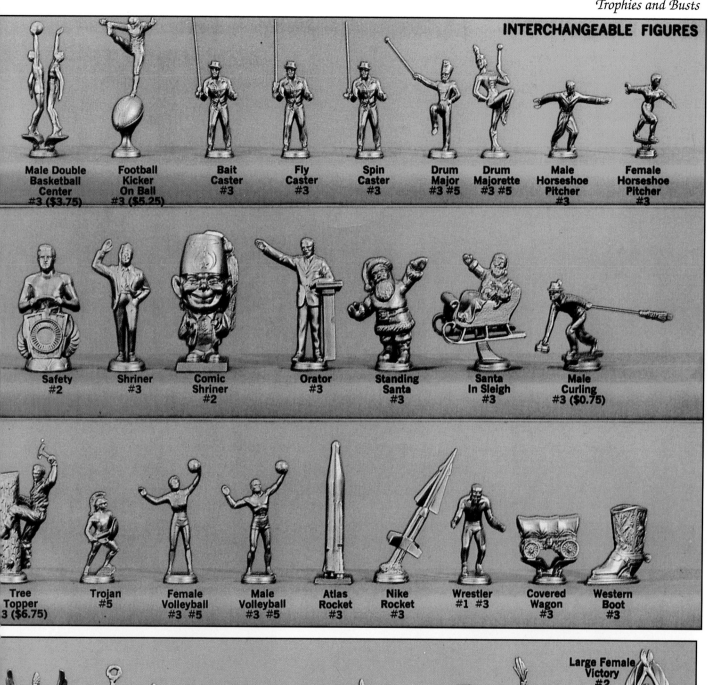

INTERCHANGEABLE FIGURES

Male Double Basketball Center #3 ($3.75) · Football Kicker On Ball #3 ($5.25) · Bait Caster #3 · Fly Caster #3 · Spin Caster #3 · Drum Major #3 #5 · Drum Majorette #3 #5 · Male Horseshoe Pitcher #3 · Female Horseshoe Pitcher #3

Safety #2 · Shriner #3 · Comic Shriner #2 · Orator #3 · Standing Santa #3 · Santa In Sleigh #3 · Male Curling #3 ($0.75)

Tree Topper 3 ($6.75) · Trojan #5 · Female Volleyball #3 #5 · Male Volleyball #3 #5 · Atlas Rocket #3 · Nike Rocket #3 · Wrestler #1 #3 · Covered Wagon #3 · Western Boot #3

Female Victory #1 #3 #4 #5 #6 #7 · Male Victory #1 #2 #3 #4 #6 #7 · Mod. Male Victory #3 #4 #5 #7 · Fem. Victory With Torch #3 · Male Victory With Torch #3 · Fem. Victory With Cup #3 · Large Male Victory Discontinued · Large Female Victory #2

Page 49

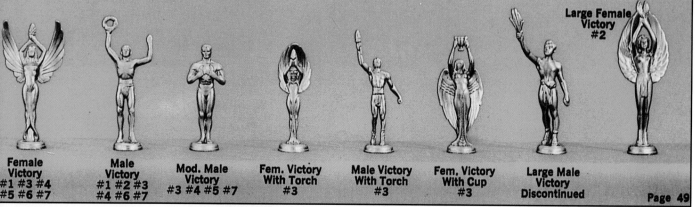

Kaag Trophies sold trophy components to the industry. This picture of a catalog sheet shows many of Don's designs. The 33 figures shown here are but a small sampling of the many figures he designed over the years.

The original waxes discovered in a box in his studio give a sampling of some of the many figures designed for trophy companies around the country.

Picture of the mid-sized
Emmy he redesigned.

The many busts of famous individuals would cause any one individual to be star struck. The list goes from political leaders to entertainment personalities to the neighbor kids down the street. Don was telling me stories of the people he met and I was getting goose bumps just sitting in his presence. Here are a few examples of the busts created and some of the places you can go to view them.

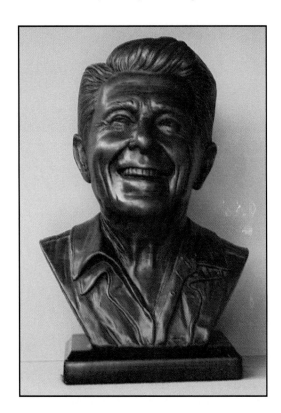

President Ronald Reagan at the Reagan Library.

Alexis DeToqueville at the United Way
Headquarters in Alexandria, Virginia.

Ze'ev Jabotinski at the Jabotinski Institute in Tel Aviv, Israel.

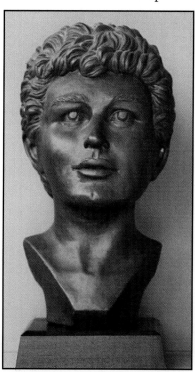

Young King David of Israel. This is held in private collections and Don Winton's home.

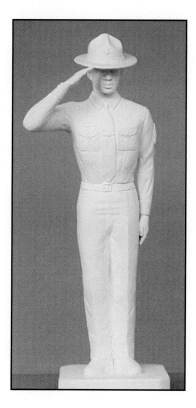

Marine Drill Instructor created for sale on the air base at El Toro, California.

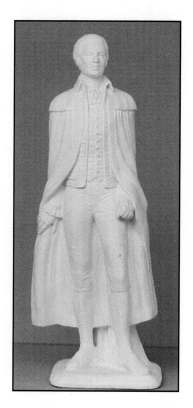

Haym Salomon held in private collections and Don Winton's home.

Simeon holding baby Jesus. One of two decorated pieces owned by Geneva Owen of Costa Mesa, California.

Simeon holding baby Jesus in bisque. Held in private collections and Don Winton's home.

Bar Mitzvah Boy in bisque. Held in private collections and Don Winton's home.

Moses in bisque. Held in private collection and Don Winton's home.

General Dolittle.
Three times life-size at March Air Force Base, California.

Captain Bruce Winton at Don's house.

David Ben Gurion at Ben Gurion
University in Tel Aviv, Israel.

General Dolittle in bisque at Don's house.

There are many others such as the Bob Hope figure in Las Vegas, Nevada, and the twelve stations of the cross on the church in Los Angeles, California. I am going to register these with the Smithsonian Institute over the next year and would appreciate your help if you have heard of one or know where one is located of which I may not be aware.

MINIATURE ANIMALS

Don's love of animals and the whimsical side of life is expressed in these wonderful little creations. None of these are marked and were sold by H & L Sales Company. For reference of size, the Scotty Dog pictured in the bottom right corner of the sales sheet is only 1" tall. On the other sales sheet the beaver laying down (second row, second from left) is 1" tall and 2½" long. All of these are between 1" and 2½".

Twin Winton Miniatures – Original Sales Flyer
#450 w/blk.-brn. spots – $11.00, #450 all brown – $11.00, #404 – $9.00, #405 – $9.00, #103 – $4.00, #313 – $6.00, #304 – $10.00, #312 – $8.00, #102 – $5.00, #106 – $5.00, #311 – $8.00, #403 – $9.00, #310 – $9.00, #406 – $11.00, #402 – $15.00, #207 – $6.00, #208 – $6.00, #204 – $6.00, #105 black or white – $4.00.

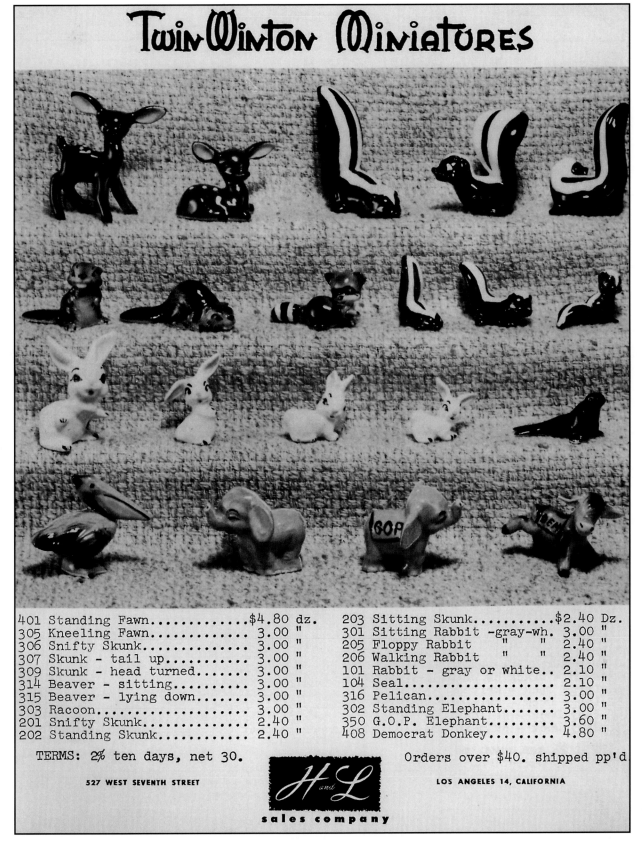

Twin Winton Miniatures

401 Standing Fawn................$4.80 dz.	203 Sitting Skunk.............$2.40 Dz.
305 Kneeling Fawn.............. 3.00 "	301 Sitting Rabbit -gray-wh. 3.00 "
306 Snifty Skunk.............. 3.00 "	205 Floppy Rabbit " " 2.40 "
307 Skunk - tail up.......... 3.00 "	206 Walking Rabbit " " 2.40 "
309 Skunk - head turned....... 3.00 "	101 Rabbit - gray or white.. 2.10 "
314 Beaver - sitting.......... 3.00 "	104 Seal..................... 2.10 "
315 Beaver - lying down....... 3.00 "	316 Pelican.................. 3.00 "
303 Racoon.................... 3.00 "	302 Standing Elephant........ 3.00 "
201 Snifty Skunk............. 2.40 "	350 G.O.P. Elephant.......... 3.60 "
202 Standing Skunk........... 2.40 "	408 Democrat Donkey.......... 4.80 "

TERMS: 2% ten days, net 30.

Orders over $40. shipped pp'd

527 WEST SEVENTH STREET

H and L

sales company

LOS ANGELES 14, CALIFORNIA

Twin Winton Miniatures – Original Sales Flyer
#401 – $11.00, #305 – $9.00, #306 – $7.00, #307 – $7.00, #309 – $7.00, #314 – $8.00, #315 – $8.00,
#303 – $8.00, #201 – $5.00, #202 – $5.00, #203 – $5.00, #301 – $9.00, #205 – $7.00, #206 – $6.00,
#101 – $4.00, #104 – $5.00, #316 – $9.00, #302 – $7.00, #350 – $20.00, #408 – $20.00.

THE TWIN WINTON MINIATURES

527 WEST SEVENTH ST.
LOS ANGELES 14, CALIF.

HL SALES COMPANY

Date _____

Ship to _____

_____

_____

Salesman: _____

Terms 2-10 Net 30

ITEM	Quan-tity	Price Dozen	Total	ITEM	Quan-tity	Price Dozen	Total
101 RABBIT Gray or White		2.10		303 RACOON		3.60	
102 BABY DUCK Yellow		2.10		304 LARGE DUCK White		3.00	
103 PIG		2.10		305 KNEELING FAWN		3.00	
104 SEAL		2.10		306 SNIFTY SKUNK		3.60	
105 SCOTTY White or Black		2.10		307 SKUNK Tail up		3.60	
106 BABY DUCK Swimming, yellow		2.10		309 SKUNK Head turned		3.60	
201 SNIFTY SKUNK		3.00		310 BURRO Sitting		3.00	
202 STANDING SKUNK		3.00		311 BURRO Lazy		3.00	
203 SITTING SKUNK		3.00		312 LARGE DUCK Swimming, White		3.00	
204 KITTY Gray or White & Black		2.40		313 SWAN Black or White		3.00	
205 FLOPPY RABBIT Gray or White		2.40		314 BEAVER Sitting		3.00	
206 WALKING RABBIT Gray or White		2.40		315 BEAVER Lying Down		3.00	
207 MOUSE Gray or White		2.40		316 PELICAN		3.00	
208 BLIND MOUSE Gray or White		2.40		317 MARE		3.00	
301 SITTING RABBIT Gray or White		3.00		318 SMALL SQUIRREL		3.00	
302 STANDING ELEPHANT		3.00		319 HEN		3.00	

Twin Winton Miniatures – Original Order Form.

ITEM	Quantity	Price Dozen	Total	ITEM	Quantity	Price Dozen	Total
320 ROOSTER		3.60		501 GNOME Fishing on toadstool		12.00	
401 STANDING FAWN		4.80		502 GNOME Fishing standing on leaf		9.60	
402 MOUSE With Yellow or Green		4.80		503 GNOME Smoking pipe on toadstool		12.00	
403 BURRO Kicking		4.50		504 GNOME Smoking pipe on leaf		9.60	
404 CALF		4.80		505 SLEEPY GNOME on toadstool		10.80	
405 RAM		4.80		506 SLEEPY GNOME on leaf		8.40	
406 BURRO With Cart		4.80		601 MINIATURE ANGEL		5.40	
407 BURRO With Hat		4.80		602 BOY ANGEL		9.60	
408 COLT		4.80		603 GIRL ANGEL		9.60	
409 LARGE SQUIRREL		4.20		701 LARGE MOUSE With Top Hat		9.00	
410 LARGE SQUIRREL Running		4.20		702 LARGE MOUSE With Sweater		9.00	
411 COUNTRY MOUSE		4.80		703 LARGE MOUSE In overalls		9.00	
450 COW Black & Brown Spots		6.00		704 LARGE MOUSE With Pipe		9.00	
451 BULL		6.00		456 SANTA White		6.00	
452 STALLION		6.00					
453 DEER Brown or White		5.40					
454 SLEIGH Brown or White		6.00					
455 SANTA Red		7.20					

Prices are wholesale, F.O.B., Pasadena, Calif. Orders for $50.00 and up shipped Prepaid.

Twin Winton Miniatures – Original Order Form.

#450 Cow
all brown, 2" tall, $11.00.

#304 Large Duck
2¼" tall, $10.00.

#208 Blind Mouse
¾" tall, $6.00.

#105 Scotty
1" tall, $4.00.

#317 Mare
1" tall, $7.00.

#311 Burro Lazy
2" tall, $8.00.

#309 Skunk Head Turned
¾" tall at tail, $7.00.

#301 Sitting Rabbit
2" tall, $9.00.

#318 Small Squirrel, brown
1¾" tall, $8.00.

#315 Beaver Lying Down
1" tall x 2½" long, $8.00.

#203 Sitting Skunk
¾" tall, $5.00.

I am very sure I have passed by these treasures in antique stores many times. I found these in San Diego when I went to visit Ross Winton's son. Now that I know what I am looking for, I am sure I will add some to my collection.

EARLY ANIMALS

The animals of Don Winton have always had a charm and creativity that is unique to this profoundly creative man. In this chapter I have listed some of the wonderful treasures created including some of the very earliest pieces. As you come across these and others I hope you collect and share your treasures with as much enjoyment as I have found.

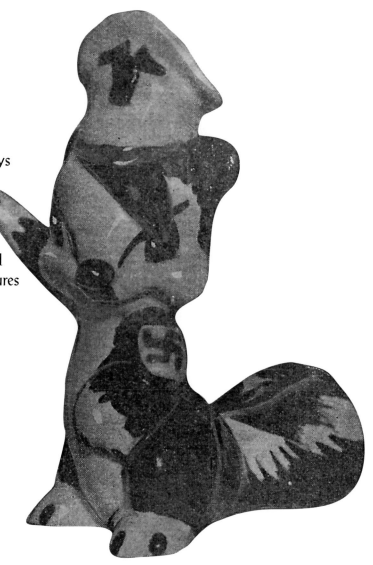

The skunk with swastika was created in the late 1930s. Approximately 3", value is undetermined as of yet because we have only found two. (One sold at auction in August 1997 for $200.00.)

Roaring Lion
airbrushed decorating method, 8", $60.00.

Archival photo strip showing 9" squirrels and 12" rabbits.
Also a duck, granny, and girl figurine not seen for a long time.

Rabbit, dated 1940 – 1943
6", $45.00.

Standing Deer, dated 1940 – 1943
6", $75.00.

Squirrel with Mallet, dated 1940 – 1943
3" x 5", $40.00.

Standing Deer with bottom showing stock #208, $95.00.

Deer Laying Down,
dated 1940 – 1943
3" x 5", $75.00.

Squirrel with Mallet
3" x 5", 40.00.

Chipmunk with Arms Extended
2" high, $20.00.

Squirrel with Folded Hands
2½" x 4", $30.00.

Squirrel Salt and Pepper
2½" high, $25.00 ea.

Squirrel with Arms Extended
2½" high, $25.00.

Squirrel Scratching Head
2½" high, $25.00.

Squirrel Holding Stomach
2½" x 4", $30.00.

Squirrel Looking Sideways
2½" x 4", $30.00.

Cat Holding Paw Up in the Air
3" high, $30.00.

Cat Standing on Hind Legs
3", $30.00.

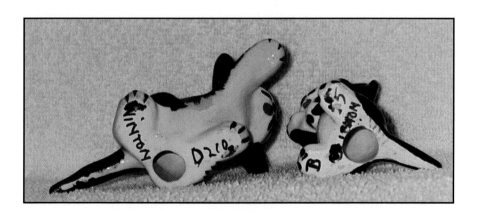

Markings on the bottom of the cats.

Sugar Puss comes in pink, blue, and green that have been currently seen. The two green cats are Sugar Puss. The black cat in the middle is a figure that has been shown earlier.
5" Sugar Puss, $50.00.

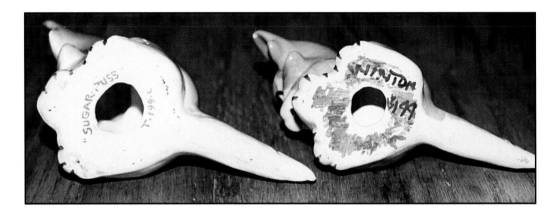

Markings on Sugar Puss. Note that one was airbrushed and one hand decorated.

3 Skunk Salt and Pepper Shakers
2½" high, $30.00 ea.

Cat	Zebra	Chipmunk in Top Hat
3", $30.00.	5", $45.00.	3", $40.00.

Snoopy Bear Bud Vase
3" x 4", $65.00.

Bottom of Snoopy.

Bear with Flowers Mug, personalized
5" high, $100.00.

Elephant Mug
3½" x 5", $125.00.

Squirrel Handle Mug
5", $100.00.

Rabbit Crouching Beside Basket Planter
5" x 8", $85.00.

Rabbit Planter with cart broken off
and missing.
7", $30.00 as is (complete $85.00).

Rabbit with Eggshell Planter
6" x 8", $85.00.

Rabbit bank, re-created by Don of old one
which had broken, 7" high, $40.00.

Rabbit with Cart
7" x 10", $85.00.

Rabbit Crouching Beside Basket Eating Carrot
5" x 8", $85.00.

Archival photo of Raccoon next to stump, dated
August 22,1954. Anyone have one of these?

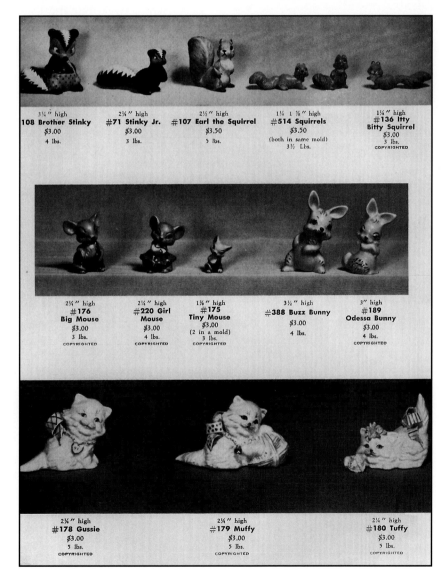

3¼" high	2¼" high	2½" high	1¼ 1⅞" high	1¼" high
108 Brother Stinky	**#71 Stinky Jr.**	**#107 Earl the Squirrel**	**#514 Squirrels**	**#136 Itty Bitty Squirrel**
$3.00	$3.00	$3.50	$3.50	$3.00
4 lbs.	3 lbs.	5 lbs.	(both in same mold) 3½ Lbs.	3 lbs. COPYRIGHTED

2¼" high	2¼" high	1⅜" high	3½" high	3" high
#176 Big Mouse	**#220 Girl Mouse**	**#175 Tiny Mouse**	**#388 Buzz Bunny**	**#189 Odessa Bunny**
$3.00	$3.00	$3.00	$3.00	$3.00
3 lbs. COPYRIGHTED	4 lbs.	(2 in a mold) 3 lbs. COPYRIGHTED	4 lbs.	4 lbs. COPYRIGHTED

2¼" high	2¼" high	2¼" high
#178 Gussie	**#179 Muffy**	**#180 Tuffy**
$3.00	$3.00	$3.00
5 lbs. COPYRIGHTED	5 lbs. COPYRIGHTED	5 lbs. COPYRIGHTED

Alberta Molds sales flier showing other pieces that were designed by Don.
Some of these may have been produced by Twin Winton before they were sold to the home artist.

CHILDREN, GNOMES and ELVES, GODEY FIGURINES

Don and Ross wanted to make a line of children figurines that looked similar to the Hummel figurines on the market. Therefore they came up with "The Childrens' Album."

A REAL CHILDREN'S ALBUM is this endearing series of carefully sculptured figures taken right from childhood.

The byline from this clipping from a 1950 L.A. Times describes the line extremely well as you will be able to see from the following examples.

Ice Skating Boy with hang tag for line 5", $175.00.

Bottom of Ice Skating Boy.

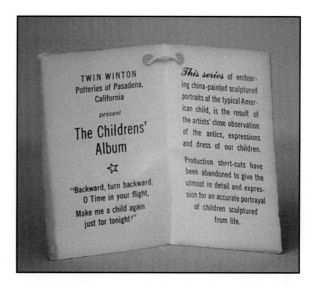

Front and back of hang tag showing the line was made in Pasadena, California.

On the inside of the hang tag it describes the intent of the line. It should be noted that this line was not extremely successful and the molds were eventually sold to Alberta Molds for the home artists.

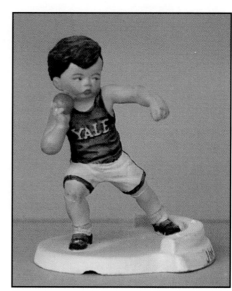

Boy Skier
7" high, $225.00.

Boy Shot Putting with Stanford
logo on chest.
(He is missing his base.)
3" high, $100.00.

Boy Shot Putting with
Yale logo on chest.
3" high, $150.00.

Bottom of Boy Shot Putting with Yale logo on chest. The marking shows the arched Twin Winton logo on the early pieces.

Football Player and Girl
5" x 6", $275.00.

Archival picture of a Cowboy. We think it is about 8" to 10" tall.

All of these have the arched Twin Winton logo on the bottom.
From left to right:

Girl Holding Arm
5" high, $175.00.

Quarterback with Green Jersey
4½" high, $175.00.

Cowboy on Stick Horse
5¼" high, $200.00.

Quarterback with Red Jersey
4½" high, $175.00.

Sample made for a local businessman.
There is only one or two of these in existence.
3" high, $85.00.

Angel Blowing Golden Trumpet
(new piece created in the early 1990s)
5" high, $40.00.

Raggedy Ann Sitting on L for Love Chair
(samples made for Alberta Molds)
8" high, $35.00.

Girl Holding Raggedy Ann and Teddy Bear
(samples for Alberta)
6½" x 6½", $45.00.

Kissing Angel Girl (sample)
8", $40.00.

A picture out of the Alberta Molds catalogs. Keep your eyes open, these may show up with the Twin Winton mark as well. I don't know for sure. If you do find any of these delightful little children I would love to see them.

Boy on Stick Horse and his Dog (made in the 1980s as part of the line for a local store in California) 6" high, $35.00.

CERAMICHROME TECHNIQUE NO. 80/25¢

Ceramichrome Scores Again!

Cover from the Ceramichrome Catalog again showing the variety of pieces that Don designed.

A line of pottery sold at Maranatha Village in Costa Mesa, California in the mid 1970s. Shekinah China was not a big seller but the pieces are wonderful. This is the dealer plaque. 5" x 7", $100.00.

Shepherd Boy
(note that the staff is also porcelain)
9" high, $80.00.

Little Girl Playing with Teddy
4" high, $35.00.

Angel on Cloud Playing Flute
6" high, $40.00.

Angel Playing Flute
4" high, $35.00.

The line of Godey figurines was not long lasting and were eventually sold to Alberta Molds. There were originally six designs but I could only locate five of them.

Godey in Gray with Red Bow and Muff
2½", $70.00 (Twin Winton),
$25.00 (Alberta).

Godey in Layered Pink Gown
2½", $60.00 (Twin Winton),
$25.00 (Alberta).

Godey in Green with Black
Bow and Purse
2½", $70.00 (Twin Winton),
$25.00 (Alberta).

Godey in Pink with Hands in Front
2½", $60.00 (Twin Winton),
$25.00 (Alberta).

Godey in Light Blue with Hands in Front
2½", $60.00 (Twin Winton),
$25.00 (Alberta).

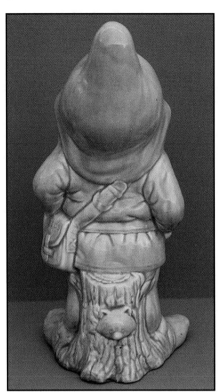

The gnomes have been a part of Don's creative genius from the time he created his first ones in Busch Gardens when he was only 17 years old. They are literally scattered up and down the years in Twin Winton and other companies. They come in all sizes and doing all kinds of jobs. This particular gnome I found at a swap meet in Santa Ana, California. The decorating method looks to be that of Bowermeister from the late Twin Winton years. I believe these are just now coming into their own and will definitely be a part of collections in the future. 13", $25.00.

There was an entire line of elves that I have discovered and am looking for more! This charming line of imaginary creatures will jump out from anywhere. This one standing on a leaf with a watering can is a good example of the mischievousness of his creator Don Winton. There is no marking on the bottom of this one to identify it. I did however confirm with Don that these are his and they were created in the years from 1950 to 1952. 5", $80.00.

Elf in Stump 3", $60.00.

Elf Holding Birthday Cake
6", only one known to exist.

lf sitting with Hands Behind
Him (unglazed)
5½", $150.00.

Elf in Shoe
6", $120.00.

Pan Sitting on Stump
6½", $100.00.

lf with Basket on his Back
3", $65.00.

Elf on Snail
5", $100.00.

Elf on Turtle
5", $75.00.

HANNA BARBERA, DISNEY, ADVERTISING

In this chapter I wanted to share some of the items that I ran across that kept reminding me of memories from my childhood. Remember Yogi Bear and his sidekick BooBoo! The Mickey Mouse telephone I wanted because it was Mickey!

Woody Woodpecker and Bob's Big Boy were part of my happy days as a kid. In looking through the photographs and collected pieces of family members and collectors I discovered that Don was very involved in all of these. The following pictures are only a small sampling of the pieces he created for the companies that owned these characters.

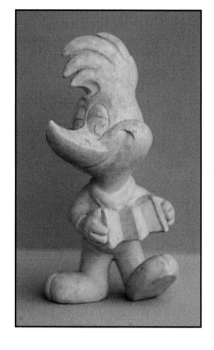

Woody Woodpecker
original wax
5", $150.00.

Archival photograph of Woody Woodpecker and giggling mouse. The ruler behind these show the height.

Yogi Bear sitting on a stump.
original wax for bottle 5",
$150.00; bottle, $18.00.

Pixie & Dixie in shoe, made for Idea Inc.
6", $75.00.

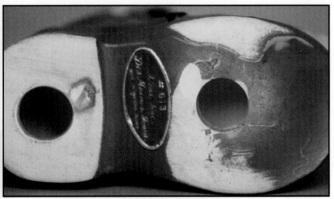

Huckleberry Hound
made for Idea Inc.
6", $50.00.

Yogi Bear sitting on a
stump. 5", $150.00.

Wally Gator bisque
6", $80.00.

BooBoo Bear
made for Idea Inc.
4", $75.00.

Yogi Bear
made for Idea Inc.
6", $60.00.

Quick Draw McGraw
made for Idea Inc.
7", $75.00.

Pixie Mouse
made for Idea Inc.
4", $50.00.

Baba Loo
made for Idea Inc.
5½", $60.00.

Snagglepuss
made for Idea Inc.
6", $60.00.

Fox
Made for Idea Inc.
6", $60.00.

Disney Corporation does not allow just any artist to work for them. They must be some of the best and most creative in the world. They also must be able to work as a team member to help come up with the perfect design to maintain the Disney image and characters. Making Mickey Mouse into a telephone that was acceptable to Disney and the consumer was no

small task and Don Winton certainly rose to the occasion. He enjoyed the challenge and looks with pride at the finished product. (This piece was offered in The Disney Corporate Gift catalog this year. You might want to order a new one for $125.00 and keep it in the original box.)

Miniature bisque of the
Mickey Mouse Telephone.
One of a kind sample.
8", $150.00.

Mickey Mouse Telephone
14", $125.00 (touchtone), 14",
$175.00 (dial).

THE NEW YORK TIMES, THURSDAY, JANUARY 3, 1980   C11

Design Notebook | Paul Goldberger

The new telephones make the old one look great by comparison.

H OW commonplace, how boring an object, the telephone. It looks plain, unthought about, fairly ordinary — there is nothing handsome about that box with a sloping front and a set of buttons and a curving thing hanging from it that you are expected to put into your hand. It would not be hard, you might think at first glance, to design a much better object that could do all of the same things.

For the last couple of years, a lot of people have been trying to go the telephone one better — including the telephone company itself. As a way of keeping up with the intense pressure from private phone makers, newly permitted access to the home telephone market, it has been offering a whole line of fancy telephones. We deserve something better than the plain old phone, the American Telephone and Telegraph Company has been telling us, and here it is.

Or here it is not. The new telephones, with a couple of pleasing exceptions, are generally wretched — neither attractive as objects of design nor practical as objects of function. Most of them prove only one thing: that the standard telephone, designed for A.T.&T. by Henry Dreyfus & Associates, is not a bad piece of design at all. Indeed, it is superb — it is easy to use, it feels comfortable to hold, it is unpretentious and matter-of-fact in appearance.

Most of the new A.T.&T. phones, which the company markets under the rubric Design Line telephones, are none of these things. They tend to be showy, rather silly objects, and in all but a few cases they are completely impractical. They result from the same esthetic fallacy — looks over practicality — that motivated the Trimline phone that A.T.&T. introduced a few years ago, the sleek, curving phone that is extremely difficult to hold and awkward to use. But at least the Trimline is a good-looking object: most of the new phones A.T.&T. makes (as well as most of the ones marketed by its competitors) are not even fun to look at.

Take, for example, the Stowaway,

One of the best designs is a lighthearted Mickey Mouse telephone

which A.T.&T. describes as "a chest in Mediterranean-style carved finish with gold-colored trim or oiled-walnut veneer with silver-colored trim." It is available for a $115 extra charge, and it is a box of fake wood in which is set a telephone that looks something like the Princess telephone, A.T.&T.'s equally impractical early attempt to lure telephone users away from the commonsense standard telephone.

The Stowaway seems designed to go perfectly with the "Mediterranean" kitchens in new East Side high-rise apartments or suburban tract housing developments. Surprisingly, it, like the

standard telephone models, was designed by the venerable firm of Henry Dreyfuss — which also produced for A.T.&T. something futuristic called the Telstar, a telephone set into a clear plastic cylinder.

The Telstar looks something like a clock radio or, from a distance, like a plastic breadbox. The clear plastic top rolls back, revealing a silver-colored panel on which is set a dial or a set of Touch-Tone buttons. From this Buck Rogers control panel the telephone user can pick up a handset containing the ear and mouthpieces, which looks more or less like a conventional telephone's

handset — save for the fact that the ear and mouthpieces are somewhat reduced in size and squared off. This makes them look more futuristic, and far less comfortable to hold and to use.

But it is not comfort we are concerned about in this brave new world of advanced telephone design. For the really daring futurist, there is something, also designed by Dreyfuss, called the Sculptura, which A.T.&T.'s brochure describes as "sleek and modern as a fine piece of sculpture in brown, white and yellow." What the Sculptura is, in fact, is a rounded form, with a base containing a dial and a handset that slides upward from it in a single swooping curve, so that the base and the handset all appear to be a single piece. It looks like a bad dream of Brancusi. The phone company reports that this one is a strong seller, perhaps because of the price, which is only $67.50. But this phone is not a bargain functionally: for the sake of the curve, the handset has been contorted into a particularly awkward position.

More promising is A.T.&T.'s newest offering, the Country Junction telephone, which premiered, so to speak, last month. This telephone, also designed by Henry Dreyfuss & Associates, attempts to take advantage of the nostalgia market, and does so fairly intelligently. We all have a romantic image of the country kitchen, with its old telephone box on the wall and a crank for ringing up Central; here is a real telephone with a modern dial and exposed bells on a wooden box, all with a handset that has been cleverly designed to look at first glance like one of those loose earpieces that old phones had. This one seems both practical and decent-looking. And, wonder of wonders, the cabinet is made of real oak.

Several of the new telephones on the market were designed and manufactured by the American Telecommunications Corporation, although they are also sold by A.T.&T. Two of these are among the best — the Mickey Mouse (a top seller) and the Snoopy and Woodstock telephones. Each has a base containing a dial or Touch Tone buttons on which the cartoon character stands. He holds in his upraised arm the standard telephone handset, making these phones practical to use.

Neither of these phones pretends to high art — they are both lighthearted objects of fantasy. But they are far more pleasing than such other American Telecommunications offerings as the Early American, Mediterranean and Antique Gold telephones, all variations on the same model, something resembling the old-style French telephones in which an ornate handset is set on a holder above a boxy base. The base and holder are covered with the appropriate design motif — an eagle in

On futuristic Sculptura model, curved handset proves hard to use.

New Country Junction model, in real oak, is both nostalgic and practical.

the case of the Early American telephone, a lot of fake gold carving in the case of the Antique Gold. It's a $135 phone that looks like part of a set for the boudoir scene in a B movie.

This trio proves one thing, however, and it is not insignificant. It seems as if the phone company is at last learning what Detroit has known all along — that there is great economy in marketing different kinds of trim on the same body. Ironically, these three phones, silly and pretentious as they are with their "maple look" and "gold-plated trim," are in fact fairly functional. They have comfortable handsets and they are heavy enough not to fall off a shelf if given a tug.

There are more — the Noteworthy, for example, designed by the Dreyfuss firm, is a Trimline phone set into the side of a plastic cabinet containing a blackboard on its front and space for a

telephone book inside. At $83, it's a bit much to pay for a blackboard, and it carries all of the shortcomings of the regular Trimline telephone, but that aside, it's not a bad-looking household object.

Far different is the Exeter, in which a telephone handset like the awkward Telstar handset is set onto a "dark brown base with simulated alligator overlay," or, for those who prefer something else, "a white base with etched-metal overlay." These look cheap and false, objects pretending to be what they are not; they have none of the pleasure of fantasy that makes the Mickey Mouse or Country Junction phones so appealing. They are just imitations of high-quality objects, whose cheapness, alas, shows all too well. They remind us anew of how decent the plain old standard telephone really is.

In January 1980, the NEW YORK TIMES featured the new Mickey Mouse Telephone in an article by Paul Goldberger.

Don has worked on a freelance basis with the Disney Corporation from the time he was a young man to the present day. In the mid 1950s he was commissioned to design all of the Hagen-Renaker figurines for Disney characters. I am looking for samples of the many designs that he put out but have not found them yet. Some of the designs I have found I am sure you will be interested in seeing.

Pirates
Limited edition of 500 each made for the opening of Pirates of the Caribbean. 8", $200.00.

Donald Duck
sample never sold
6", $150.00.

Dumbo Cookie Jar sample
12", $250.00.

Sam the Eagle
12", $200.00.

Don working on the design of Mickey the Sorcerer in his studio.

Mickey the Sorcerer
8", $150.00.

Little Mermaid sample
6", $75.00.

Tinkerbell, bisque
6", $75.00.

Jimney Cricket
6", $80.00.

Pinocchio
8", $100.00.

Winnie the Pooh, bisque
5", $60.00.

Mickey the Apprentice
bisque, 7", $75.00.

Sleeping Beauty Castle
sample, only two cast
6", $200.00.

Pinocchio, Pluto, and Bambi. Original wax for the Disney soaps.
2½", $50.00 ea.

Mickey Mouse with Open Hand
original wax
7", $200.00.

As Don's talent and reputation grew more and more people called. The advertising media sat up and took notice of the talent of Don Winton and commissioned him to do several fun pieces.

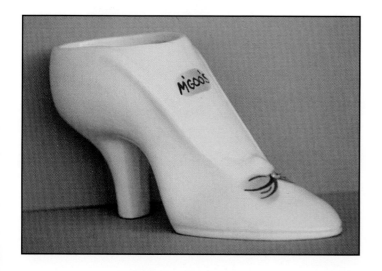

High Heel Planter
made for M'Goos Restaurant
4" high, $15.00.

Alligator Mascot
large bronze sculpture for high school in
Nevada, this is a bisque copy
8", $50.00.

Burgie Coffee Mug
5½", $40.00.

Bottom of Burgie Mug.

Oldsmobile Logo Ashtrays
made as a premium for Oldsmobile dealership
6", $15.00 ea.

Wampum Bank
made for Wampum Corn Chips as a premium
8", $85.00.

Capistrano Honey Jar
made for San Juan Mission Honey
9", $100.00.

Volkswagen Bank
made for Volkswagen dealer
5" x 8½", $125.00.

Howard Johnson's Cookie Jar. Owned by Joyce Roerig. Victor Bonomo, long-time salesman for Twin Winton, sold this to a Howard Johnson's on the Pennsalvanyia Turnpike. He told me that only 100 were ordered and produced. If you are lucky enough to find one, you have a treasure. It is marked Twin Winton on the bottom.
10" x 12", $3,000.00.

Archival photo of staff in the office in San Juan Capistrano. Notice sitting on the cabinet behind the staff the Hotei figure and the Ford Dog Bank. This led me to the other three designs of the banks. All of these were made for premiums, you got one when you bought a car from the dealer.

Ford Dog Holding Case
7", $50.00.

Ford Dog with Son
Wearing Cap
7½", $65.00.

Ford Dog with Collar
8", $55.00.

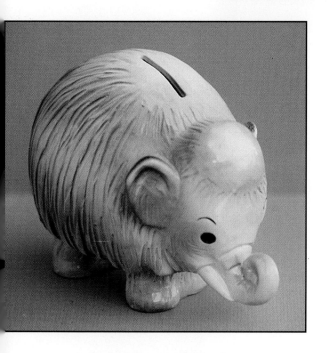

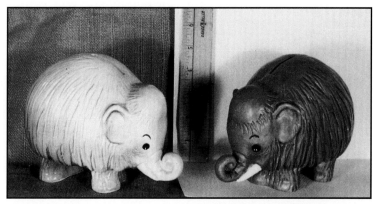

Archival photo of Wooly Mammoth. It apparently came in the wood stain and the ivory finish.

Wooly Mammoth Bank
made for Ford dealership
5", $75.00.

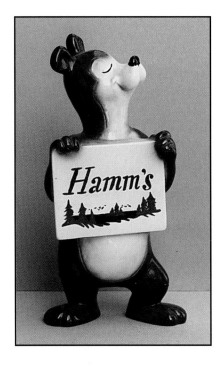

Hamm's Beer Bear Figurine
made for sample
5", $100.00.

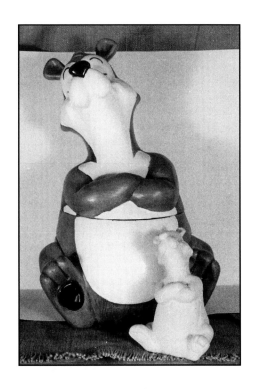

Hamm's Beer Bear Cookie Jar
sample
15", $250.00.

Bob's Big Boy Bank
approximately 250 of these were
made for distribution, marking on
the bottom is "Twin Winton @56
Made in USA"
8", $125.00.
Bob's Big Boy Cookie Jar was also
offered. Value: $250.00.

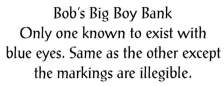

Bob's Big Boy Bank
Only one known to exist with
blue eyes. Same as the other except
the markings are illegible.

DISHES

Included in this chapter are the dish lines and miscellaneous household items such as toothpick holders, pitchers, garlic pots, chip n dip bowls, vases, and ashtrays. The three major dish lines manufactured by Twin Winton are the Bamboo Line (inspired by Joann Winton, Ross's wife), the Artists Palette Line (I named this one because of the marking on the bottom), and the B.K. Bar Line (as shown on the flier). More dish lines were designed by Don and manufactured by other companies. These will have to be dealt with at a later date.

Bamboo Line

This line also has a pitcher, planter 12" long x 5" wide x 6" high, and possibly other items of which I am not aware. The following pictures will give you an idea of the coloring and general look of the pieces.

Stein
8" tall, $35.00.

Mug
6" tall, $20.00.

Artist Palette Line

The marking on the bottom of the plates have an artist palette as part of the logo. Therefore, that is how this line is identified. (Note the giant hillbilly tankard sitting on the back of the table.)

Dinner in mid 1950s using this line.

Saucer 6" diameter,
Cup 3" diameter, $20.00 each.

Creamer
4" diameter, $40.00.

Sugar Lid
(sorry the bowl got broken)
4" diameter, $40.00 (bowl and lid).

Salt & Pepper Shaker
3½" tall, $65.00.

Salad Bowl, 13" diameter, $250.00+.
This piece is easily broken and very rare.

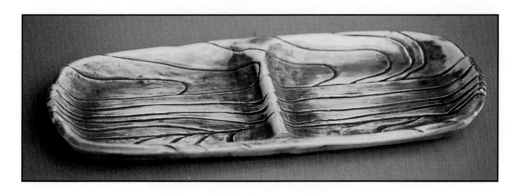

Relish Tray, 4" x 8", $30.00.

Mug, 4½", $35.00.

Mug with silver banding, 4½", $50.00.

Tumbler, 4½", $25.00.

Salad Plate, 8" diameter, $40.00.

Steak Plate
7½" x 12", $60.00.

Wood Grain Line
(Also know as the B.K. Bar Line)

Archival photo showing some
of the available pieces.

Stein with D A W (these are Don's initials)
7", $60.00. (Damaged as it is, the stein is still
valuable because of the initials.)

Dinner Plate
10", $40.00.

Mug with rope and spur handle
4" tall, $40.00.

Steins
(Note the two different colors of interior glazes. These glazes are also used in planters and other pieces. The color of glazes I have discovered so far are green, yellow, white, and brown.)

Tumblers
7" tall, $40.00.

Tumblers
(Note the two different colors of interior glazes.)

Small tumblers, 4", $20.00.

Marking on the bottom
of the tumblers.

Robert S. Barkell Co.
Established in 1930

3321-25 GROVE STREET • **BERKELEY 3, CALIFORNIA**

B/K BAR LINE

An outstanding line of rustic drinkingware and accessories by TWIN WINTON.
Exterior finish: Driftwood Grey or Driftwood Brown with canary yellow interior glaze.   TERMS: 2/10 Net 30 Days...F.O.B. Pasadena, California

Registered CALIFORNIA

BK-21	BK-20
Ash Tray 7½" Sq.	3 pc. Cigarette Set
9.00 dz	15.00 dz sets

BK-3	BK-2	BK-1	BK-13	BK-12
12 oz.Zombie	12 ozHiBall	7oz O.F.	Nut Bowl	Pretzel Bowl
6.00 dz	6.00 dz	3.60 dz	6.00 dz	18.00 dz

BK-4	BK-5	BK-10	BK-11
14 oz Mug	20 oz Stein	1 3/4 qt Pitcher	2½ qt Pitcher
7.50 dz	9.00 dz	21.00 dz	36.00 dz

LOS ANGELES SHOWROOM
527 WEST SEVENTH STREET

SAN FRANCISCO SHOWROOM
238 WESTERN MDSE. MART

Robert S. Barkell Co. was a sales company used by Twin Winton to sell this line of
dishes. The description of the decorating is listed on the top of the flier.

Top row: BK-21 Ashtray, $15.00; BK-20 Cigarette Set (Cigarette Box and 2 Ashtrays), $40.00.

Middle row: BK-312 oz. Zombie, $20.00; BK-212 oz. Hi-Ball, $20.00; BK-17 oz Old Fashioned,
$15.00; BK-13 Nut Bowl, $25.00; BK-12 Pretzel Bowl, $60.00.

Bottom row: BK-414 oz. Mug, $40.00; BK-520 oz. Stein, $50.00; BK-101 ¾ qt. Pitcher, $80.00;
BK-112 ½ qt. Pitcher, $125.00.

HILLBILLIES 1947+

When Don and Bruce got out of the service in late 1946 they decided to reopen the Twin Winton Factory. The two brothers contacted Ross and convinced him to come home and join them, which he did in 1947. Don designed the Hillbilly series which proved to be a tremendous success. In fact, the factory could barely keep up with the production.

Sistie Winton (Bruce's wife) hard at work cleaning a Hillbilly Stein in 1948. She recalls that they had to have another manufacturer help with the decorating on some of the mugs and steins.

Stein and Mug.
The mug pictured is finished in the early decorating technique. This hand detailing was quite expensive and time consuming. Note the change of texture and how much less handwork is involved in the stein. The decorator could stain the entire piece, wipe it, and then do the final detail on the handle and rings. You will discover the same decorating process was used on the entire line and then changed to the more cost effective method.

A few of these items had names on them. The names were added by Don for presents or on request by a customer. Different methods of personalization were used as the product developed.

Personalization written on the bottom.

Personalization incised on the side and painted.

Personalization in a recessed sign on the side of the piece.

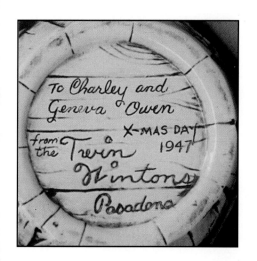

Personalization incised on the side and painted. The personalizations sometimes have dates on them. This is the earliest date I have found on a Hillbilly piece so far. This pitcher was given to Norma's sister and her husband Christmas of 1947, before Don and Norma were married in 1948. Norma thinks Don was still trying to make points to impress her. If you have located an earlier date I would love to see it.

The high sales volume lasted a little over three years as Don remembers. So most all of the production of the Hillbillies occurred between 1947 and 1951. I came across some of the original sales fliers in my research. The lines will be broken down for purposes of this book by the sales fliers available. Pieces that are not on the fliers will be listed separately in this chapter. I am sure there are pieces around that I have not included and would appreciate your help for future reference.

HILLBILLY HUMOR

The Twin Winton line is a colorful hand painted, highly decorated, and glazed assortment of California ceramics designed to pour out good cheer and add humor to bar, den, or rumpus room. It is also ideal for barbecue use and will attract many purchasers.

The famous "Twin Winton" hillbilly boys embody the spirit of true mountain humor. These carefully drawn caricatures in colorful California hand painted ceramics will fill homes with real mountain cheer.

Made in bright colors, these ceramics are eagerly sought for by the discriminating buyer seeking a distinctive collection of interesting pieces. A "Twin Winton" display in your store window will attract shoppers.

"Twin Winton" is a great "add to line." Customers will constantly repeat on both old and new items.

Item	No.	Price	Height
Stein	H-103	$21.00 Per Doz.	8"
Hillbilly Mugs	H-102	18.00 Per Doz.	5"
Hillbilly Punch Cups	H-111	9.00 Per Doz.	3"
Hillbilly Pitcher	H-101	3.50 Each	7½"
"Clem" Ash Tray	H-108	24.00 Per Doz.	3½"
Cigarette Box	H-109	24.00 Per Doz.	7"
Pretzel Bowl	H-105	2.75 Each	4½"
Salt and Pepper	H-107	12.00 Per Doz.	4"
Hillbilly Lamp	H-106	17.50 Each (complete with shade)	27"
Pouring Spout Only	H-104	12.00 Per Doz.	6½"

With an order of $50.00, a pouring spout display stand is furnished free.

5" high by 9½" wide.   Holds 6 pouring spouts.

Display sketches of these characters, pictured in their mountain retreats, are available on request. There are six different drawings on textured paper, each one in a different color. Due to the cost of these sketches, we can supply only one with each $15.00 in purchases.

Hillbilly Humor flier

Stein H-103
8" tall, $40.00.

Mugs H-102, 5", $30.00.

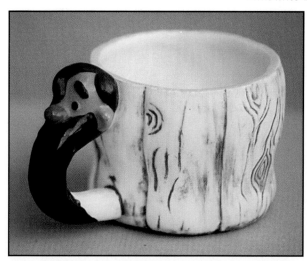

Punch Cup H-111
3", $15.00.

Pitcher H-101, 7½", $85.00.

Pitcher H-101
7½", $75.00.
(Note the more cost effective decorating
method was used on this piece.)

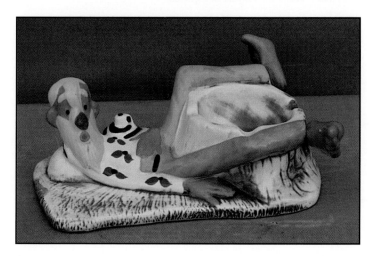

Ashtray, "Clem" H-108
3½" tall, $50.00.

Candy Dish
5¼" diameter, $75.00.

Cigarette Box, Outhouse H-109
7", $75.00.

Pretzel Bowl H-105
4½" tall, $40.00.

Salt & Pepper H-107
4", $35.00 set.

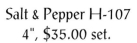

H-106

Lamp – Hillbilly with one leg down and one leg up on barrel, H-106, size 27" from the bottom of the barrel to the top of the lamp shade, $350.00.

Lamp – Hillbilly with leg crossed and leaning back slightly, 27" from the bottom of the barrel to the top of the lamp shade, $350.00. (Apparently there is more than one style of lamp out there. If you run across a different lamp than mentioned in this book, please send a picture to me.)

Lamp – Hillbilly with leg crossed but not leaning back. This design did double duty as a lamp and a keg. It is the same size as the other lamps, $350.00. (The Animals $40.00, Honey Pot $50.00, Squirrel Mug $30.00, and Hillbilly Mug $20.00 place this photo in 1949 – 1952. It also gives us an idea of the variety available at the time.)

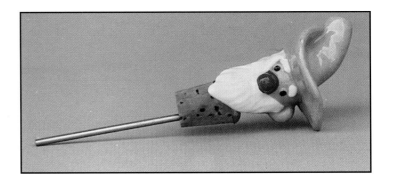

Pouring Spout H-104
6½", $25.00.

Lamp – Color picture of lamp shown
on bottom of page 113.

Pouring Spout Display
5" tall x 8½" wide, $500.00.
(Note that the Pouring Spout Display in the Hillbilly Humor
flier is actually the Bronco Group Pouring Spout display. The
Corral display is listed in the Bronco Group flier.) I have pictured the original Pouring Spout Display here.

Display sketches of characters, pictured in their mountain retreats. Six different drawings on textured paper, each one is a different color. Value – Too
rare to value. (Not known currently if any are still in existence. If available,
please let me know.)

Twin Winton
PASADENA, CALIFORNIA

MOUNTAIN HUMOR
in
ye CUP and BOWL SET

THIS VERSATILE CUP AND BOWL SET CAN BE USED FOR
MANY PURPOSES. TOM AND JERRY BOWL — PUNCH BOWL
— OR SALAD BOWL. MADE WITH ASSORTED COLORED
CUP HANDLES, THIS GLAZED CERAMIC SET WITH CARI-
CATURED MOUNTAIN FOLK WILL BRING LAUGHTER AND
CHEER TO BAR, PATIO, AND DINING ROOM.

DESCRIPTION	DIMENSIONS	PRICE
Bowl Only	12" Diameter	$ 9.00 Each
Cups Only	3" Diameter	$ 9.00 Doz.

SET OF BOWL AND 8 ASSORTED CUPS. **$13.50**

SALES OFFICE
JIMMY SMITH
ROOM 905 • BRACK SHOPS • TRinity 8568
527 WEST 7TH STREET • LOS ANGELES 14, CALIF.

Mountain Humor flier

Side one of bowl.

Side two of bowl
12" diameter, $350.00.
A unique bowl that has many uses as you can see by the flier. Developed in 1948 to go along with the cups, it was often sold as a set. The bottom of this piece reads "The Wintons, March 30, 1949 - Twin Winton Pasadena, Calif."

A set of eight punch cups went with the bowl.

1190 N. FAIR OAKS AVE.
PASADENA 3. CALIF.
SYCAMORE 8-1325

The TWIN WINTON Hillbilly Line

LADIES OF THE MOUNTAINS

Twin Wintons Hillbilly line of bar, barbecue, and rumpus room accessories is a proven seller. These quaint and laughable conversational items now have the illustrated companion pieces—a lady Hillbilly. Your old customers will want these new numbers to add to their present set.

Item	No.	Price	Height
Mug (woman)	H-102 W	$18.00 Dz.	5″
Stein (woman)	H-103 W	21.00 Dz.	8″
Spout (woman)	H-104 W	12.00 Dz.	6½″
Salt & Pepper Shakers (man & woman)	H-107	12.00 Dz. Pr.	4″
Small Ashtray	H-110 MW	9.00 Dz.	4½″x4¼′

Represented by

ROBERT S. BARKELL CO.
Offices: 3325 Grove Street • Berkeley, California
San Francisco Showroom • 238 Merchandise Mart
Los Angeles Showroom • Brack Shops, 527 West 7th Street

Ladies of the Mountains flier

This line was developed after the Hillbilly Humor line as a companion line. The items listed are limited and I am sure there will be more appearing after this book. Not as many of this line were produced and therefore they will demand a higher price if you can find them at all.

Pour Spout (woman)
6½", $30.00.

Small Ashtray (woman)
4½" x 4¼", $20.00.

Mug (woman)
5" tall, $50.00.

Ladies of the Mountain Stein
8", $70.00.

Salt & Pepper Shakers (man & woman)
4", $40.00.

Small Ashtray (man)
4½" x 4¼", $20.00.

There are a lot of things for which I do not have original sales fliers. In looking through the family photos, however, I found some archival photographs that are of interest to us all.

Don created a line of kegs for the bar that were rather unique. Here he is talking with a friend while he works on one.

Four keg designs in the warehouse with a companion display figurine of a Hillbilly resting on his arm. On the far left is a lamp base.

Keg - XXX
14" tall (including base) x 7" long, $350.00+.
(The kegs did not sell well and will be hard to locate. If you have one or know of the location of any, please let me know.)

Keg, Mountain Doo
12" tall (including base) x 8" long, $350.00+.

Hillbilly figurine for display
4" tall x 8½" long, $85.00.

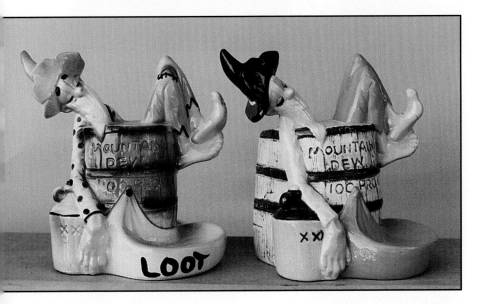

Bank, Mountain Dew Loot
7", $75.00.
(Please note that Alberta's Molds bought this design and distributed it to the home artists. The one marked "Loot" is also incised on the bottom Twin Winton. This should give you an idea of colors and the detail used by the factory.)

15" Giant gallon tankard.
(For size comparison it has been put next to a regular 7" stein.) Only one found, however, historical pictures indicate they were in production. Value: $250.00.

Bowl, Bathing Hillbilly
6" tall x 6" diameter, $40.00.

"Ezra" or "Zeke"
5½", $40.00.

(No picture available)
Wall Pocket
5" across, $80.00.

The ice buckets were listed in the catalogs 1963 through 1971. They apparently started making these while still in El Monte prior to the move to San Juan Capistrano. They all included a plastic liner that fit in the bottom of the piece. The marking on the bottom is "Twin Winton-California, USA."

Picture of liner and top.

Picture of Bottoms Up Ice Bucket.

Pictures from 1964 catalog

Ice Bucket – TW-30 "Suspenders"
7½" wide x 14" tall, $250.00.

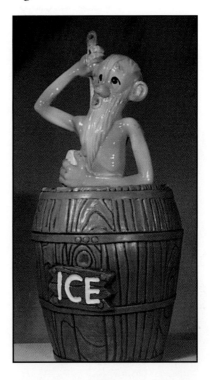

Ice Bucket – TW-31 "Bathing"
7½" wide x 16" tall, $450.00.
(This one is in catalogs 1963 through 1966 only. The other three are in the catalogs from 1963 through 1971.)

Ice Bucket – TW-32 "Bottoms Up"
7½" wide x 14" tall, $250.00.

Ice Bucket – TW-33 "With Jug"
7½" wide x 14" tall, $350.00.

HILLBILLIES 1969

These designs, modeled after the Hillbillies of earlier years, are intended to be light-hearted and encourage us to not take life so seriously. Don created these in 1969. Ross & JoAnn Winton went to Japan and negotiated with the manufacturer and placed the order.

Approval samples for Ross to sign off.

Ross Winton holding the Hillbilly mug sample.

Ross Winton at the negotiating table in Japan. (Note the familiar items on the table.)

They were ordered for and distributed by Twin Winton. When they were brought in they did not sell very well. Alma Garzo, who worked in shipping at Twin Winton, said they were not shipped out very often. They were subsequently sold at a discount. There was only one shipment of these Hillbillies from Japan. There is no exact count, but if you find one of these items you have a real treasure. To my understanding from the Wintons and the employees I have contacted, the following list is the complete line of the items brought in at that time. However, the Winton boys continue to surprise me. The marking on the bottom is an oval sticker ³⁄₁₆" x ⁷⁄₁₆" that says "Japan." No other marking is on the piece.

Pitcher with Hillbilly handle
7½" tall, $90.00.

Barrel Mug with Hillbilly handle
4" tall, $30.00.

Mustache Mug
3" tall, $50.00.
(This item did not exist in the
1950 Hillbilly series.)

Stein with Hillbilly handle
7½" tall, $50.00.

Pretzel Bowl with head on
one end and feet on the other
8½" long x 6" wide, $60.00.

Napkin Holder with Hillbilly holding jug.
5¾" tall x 6½" wide, $125.00.
(This item did not exist in the
1950 Hillbilly series.)

Salt & Pepper Shaker Barrels
(Alma Garzo, an ex-employee of Twin Winton has
this salt shaker with Twin Winton-sample, incised
into the bottom) 5" tall (both are the same height),
$45.00 set.

No picture available

Ashtray – Clem laying down with
ashtray between his legs. Same style
as the old Hillbilly "Clem."
3" tall x 6" long, $75.00.

No picture available

Ashtray – Round ashtray with picture of
PA in the bottom of the ashtray. There
could be a MA ashtray as well. Linda
Guffey found this in an antique store in
San Diego area. 2¾" x 5¼", $40.00.

Bank (back)
6½" tall, $80.00.

Bank (front)

If you find a piece that looks similar to this line, please let me know by sending me a picture of the piece. There was a display figure for this line of a Hillbilly reclining on his elbow, see if you can find it in the previous pictures. There were also three decanters ordered at the same time as these Hillbillys. You will find them in the chapter dealing with decanters.

BRONCO GROUP

This Western motif line was developed after the Hillbilly Humor line and the Ladies of the Mountain line. According to Don, the Bronco Group is one of the lines that was on the market the least. The maximum that this line was on the market was two years.

The earliest date I found on the Bronco Group was this one from Ross Winton to JoAnn, his wife, dated March 8, 1949.

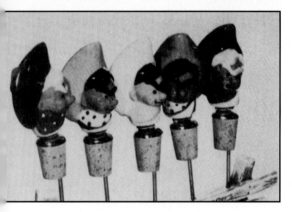

Pouring Spout B204
6¾" tall, $45.00.

Pouring Spout Display (Corral) B204 D
4¾" tall, $350.00.

Ashtray B- 208
5½" tall, $75.00.

In my research I found these two fliers that give us a line list. This sure beats looking for things that don't exist.

Twin Winton
PASADENA · CALIFORNIA

1190 N. FAIR OAKS AVE.
PASADENA 3, CALIF.
SYcamore 8-1325

The traditional West in colorful glazed ceramic can now be brought into every home with the new Bronco group by Twin Winton. These Bronco busters in Western finery and array will be a source of immediate merriment and laughter wherever they go. Prominently displayed these cowboys will sell themselves.

"Twin Winton" is a great "ADD TO LINE" customers will constantly repeat on both old and new items.

DISPLAY THESE IN YOUR WINDOW
AND WATCH THE CROWD GATHER.

ITEM	NO.	PRICE	HEIGHT	DESCRIPTION
Pouring Spout	B 204	$12.00 doz.	6¾"	
Pouring Spout Display	B 204 D	....	4¾"	No charge with $50.00 purchase. Holds 5 pouring spouts.
Ash Tray	B 208	$24.00 doz.	5½"	Large cowboy.

Represented by

Pouring Spout flier

1190 N. FAIR OAKS AVE.
PASADENA 3, CALIF.
SYcamore 8-1325

"Twin Winton" is a great "ADD TO LINE" customers will constantly repeat on both old and new items.

DISPLAY THESE IN YOUR WINDOW
AND WATCH THE CROWD GATHER.

The Twin Winton line, famous for its humorous Hill Billy Ensemble, now presents the Bronco Group, a companion line in the Western motif.

These cleverly hand painted and glazed ceramic pieces will appeal to sportsmen and outdoor lovers. These pieces in the home, bar, den, or patio will bring the colorful West to brighten up any decorative scheme.

Represented by

ITEM	NO.	PRICE	HEIGHT	DESCRIPTION
Pitcher	B 201	$ 3.50 ea.	7½"	Cowboy on handle.
Mug	B 202	18.00 doz.	4¾"	Cowboy on handle.
Stein	B 203	15.00 doz.	5"	Tree branch handle. with steer head in relief.
Punch Cups	B 211	9.00 doz.	3"	
Pretzel Bowl	B 205	2.75 ea.	5½"	Length 8".
Salt & Pepper	B 207	9.00 doz. pr.	3"	

Pitcher & Stein flier

Pitcher B 201
Cowboy on handle with bronc on pitcher. (Pictured with this pitcher are the punch cups.)
7½" tall, $125.00.

Punch Cup B 211
3" tall, $25.00.

Mug B 202
Cowboy on handle
4¾" tall, $50.00.

Stein B 203
5" tall, $70.00.
Tree branch handle with steer head in relief.

Salt & Pepper Shaker (Saddle) B207
3" tall, $50.00 set.

Pretzel Bowl B205
5½" tall x 8" long, $85.00.

In the search for success, the Wintons modified the successful Hillbillies in hopes that they might have another bonanza year. It didn't happen and so they were forced to look in other areas.

TWINTON FIGURINES

In 1971 Ross Winton and his sons (Cam and Kirk) formed Twinton Inc. It was in business until 1977 at which time they decided to shut it down. The Twinton Figures were designed by Don in 1971. Ross made a trip to Japan and ordered approximately 2,000 of each of the 20 designs. He also ordered between 200 and 300 of the display stands. They were originally sold at the J.C. Penneys stores for $2.99 each. Unfortunately, they did not sell very well and some were sold at a discount to get rid of them. Don told me he remembered seeing them for .99¢ each at a Southern California discount store.

Kirk Winton told me when the figures were delivered there were seconds. These were not sellable because the decorating was unsatisfactory. He and his brother Cam had no use for them, so they took the seconds out into the desert and used them for target practice. He said they got pretty good at blowing them up. Also upon cleaning out a storage unit after Ross passed away, Kirk said that the family took cases of the Twinton figures, catalogs, and other information to the dump. As I was told, they had two 14' trucks full of stuff that was tossed. Kirk also told me he wished he could tell the future.

The markings on the imported ones seem to be fairly uniform, a stamp on the bottom reading Twinton – 1972 and the stock number of the piece. However, some of these pieces have Twinton incised on the front of the piece. The name sometimes got sanded off the front during the cleaning of the pieces. These wonderful figures are extremely hard to find but make a delightful addition to your collection if they can be found.

T-21 - Twinton Dealer Plaque
200 to 300 ordered from Japan
5½" x 12", $400.00.

T-1 – Boy wearing Mickey Mouse
ears holding airplane and hot-dog
5½", $150.00.

No photo for this item:

T-4 – Black girl wearing Mickey Mouse ears, 5½", $150.00.

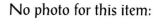

T-2 – Girl wearing Mickey Mouse ears holding sucker 5½", $150.00.

T-3 – Black boy wearing Mickey Mouse ears holding airplane and hot-dog 5½", $150.00.

T-5 – Blonde girl holding bunny 3½", $125.00.

T-6 – Girl holding sucker 5½", $150.00.

T-8 – Boy standing by mailbox 5½", $175.00.

Mystery piece – Boy standing by mailbox, 5½", value yet to be determined. (Not Twinton.)

T-9 – Black girl holding sucker
5½", $150.00.

T-10 – Black boy football player
5½", $175.00.

T-11 – Blond boy holding teddy bear
3½", $125.00.

T-12 – Girl playing in the sand
3½", $200.00.

T-13 – Black boy holding teddy bear
3½", $125.00.

T-14 – Black girl holding elephant
3½", $125.00.

T-15 – Asian boy holding frog
5½", $150.00.

T-16 – Asian girl holding books
5½", $100.00.

T-18 – Girl holding bird to nest
5½", $175.00.

T-19 – Girl playing dress-up
5½", $200.00.

No photo for these items:
T-7
T-17
T-20

I am sure you noticed the list is missing some numbers. I have a lead on the remaining pieces but was not able to get them in time for this book. If you find them before I do please give me a call so I can complete this list for us all.

TWIN WINTON COOKIE JARS

The pictures of cookie jars listed in this chapter have all been taken out of the original catalogs so you may see what was offered to the retailers through the advertising sheets. It is important to note that not all of the jars known to be Twin Winton are listed here. I was able to collect catalogs from 1961 (El Monte) through 1975 (San Juan Capistrano) with the exception of 1962, 1965, 1970, and 1973. If you have access to one of these I would love to get a copy of it.

The decorating of these jars will help you to identify the approximate year your treasure was manufactured.

Key to colors:

wf: wood finish	i: ivory	g: gray	a: avocado
p: pineapple	o: orange	r: red	

The airbrush finish (pictured here on Little Angel) with hand detailing was used very early in the company history. It was used for samples and occasionally for other pieces but does not seem to be used widespread in manufacturing process.

The wood finish (pictured here on TW-58 Pot O Cookies) was developed in the early 1950s and was continued until the company closed in 1977 – 1978. It is worth noting that the detail was normally painted in one of six colors: pink, blue, green, yellow, white, and black.

Gray finish on TW-53 Teddy Bear.

The colored finishes were developed in 1968 and showed up in the catalog in 1969. Five of the finishes, gray, avocado (green), pineapple (golden yellow), red, and orange were listed in the 1969 catalog. The ivory showed up in later catalogs but apparently was available from about the same period.

Orange finish on TW-90 Lion.

Red finish on TW-38 Pot Bellied Stove.

Avocado finish on TW-84 Bear.

Pineapple finish on TW-97 Cookie Shack.

Ivory finish on TW-57 Cookie Elf.

The collector series decoration jars were made in 1974 through 1976. When Mr. Bowermeister purchased the business, he discontinued decorating in this method because it was too costly. You can find this method of decorating in the chapter listed "Collector Series."

Tan finish under glaze pictured here on TW-84 Bear was developed right near the closing of Twin Winton. Mr. Bowermeister was manufacturing pieces with this finish which meant the piece was made around 1976 to 1978.

It is important to note that Bruce Winton was an extremely sharp businessman and whenever a salesman called in an order or special decorating request he would do almost anything to fill that request. Also employees were allowed to decorate their own pieces for themselves and as gifts. Because of this information you should keep your eyes wide open for any design in any finish from cookie jars to wall pockets, mugs to dealer plaques. You never know what you will find when you are looking for these pieces.

This is part of the reason that the collecting of Don's pieces are so fascinating. If you match the design with the approximate size listed in this book you can be sure you have a Don Winton design. If you want to be sure it is a Twin Winton manufactured piece you must also verify it by the finishes listed in this book.

TW-35 Apple
Size: 8" x 11"
Weight: 3.04 lbs.
Colors: wf-i-g-a-p-o-r
Catalog(s): 1971, 1972
Value: $180.00

TW-67 Baker
Size: 7" x 11"
Weight: 3.08 lbs.
Colors: wf
Catalog(s): 1966
Value: $400.00

TW-54 Bambi
Size: 8" x 10"
Weight: 3.10 lbs.
Colors: wf-i-g-a-p-o-r
Catalog(s): 1963, 1964, 1966, 1967,
1968, 1969, 1971, 1972, 1974
Value: $175.00

COOKIE BARN

NUMBER	**TW 41**
SIZE	8 x 12
WEIGHT	4.00 lbs

PRICES

WOOD FINISH	3.50
IN COLOR (A-P-O-R)	4.00

(Individually Boxed)

TW-41 Barn
Size: 8" x 12"
Weight: 4.00 lbs.
Colors: wf-i-g-a-p-o-r
Catalog(s): 1967, 1968, 1969, 1971,
1972, 1974, 1975
Value: $80.00
Note: Also listed under canisters.

BARREL

NUMBER	**TW 62**
SIZE	7 ¼ x 9
WEIGHT	3.06 lbs

PRICE: 3.50

**IN
WOOD FINISH**

(Individually Boxed)

BUTLER

NUMBER	**TW 60**
SIZE	7 ¼ x 12
WEIGHT	3.04 lbs

PRICE: 3.50

**IN
WOOD FINISH**

(Individually Boxed)

TW-60 Butler
Size: 7¼" x 12"
Weight: 3.04 lbs.
Colors: wf-i-g-a-p-o-r
Catalog(s): 1964, 1966, 1967, 1968, 1969
Value: $300.00

TW-62 Barrel
Size: 7¼" x 9"
Weight: 3.06 lbs.
Colors: wf
Catalog(s): 1964, 1966, 1967, 1968
Value: $75.00
Note: There is an earlier version of this without the mouse finial.

TW-84 Bear
Size: 7" x 12"
Weight: 3.12 lbs.
Colors: wf-i-g-a-p-o-r
Catalog(s): 1963, 1964, 1966, 1967, 1968, 1969, 1971, 1972, 1974, 1975
Value: $50.00
Note: Common name is Ranger Bear. The rarer jar looks the same with the addition of a badge. Double the value for this jar.

TW-58 Bird's Nest (no photo available)
Colors: wf
Catalog(s): 1969
Too rare to value.
Note: This is listed on 1969 memo as one that went out to salesmen. It was not in any catalog. Some were sold locally in San Juan Capistrano, California.

COOKIE CAR

NUMBER	**TW 98**
SIZE	7 x 12
WEIGHT	4.00 lbs

PRICES

WOOD FINISH   3.50

IN COLOR
(A-P-O-R)   4.00

(Individually Boxed)

TW-98 Cable Car
Size: 7" x 12"
Weight: 4.00 lbs.
Colors: wf-i-g-a-p-o-r
Catalog(s): 1969, 1971, 1972, 1974, 1975
Value: $75.00

CHILD IN SHOE

NUMBER	**TW 82**
SIZE	10 x 11
WEIGHT	3.12 lbs

PRICE: 3.50

**IN
WOOD FINISH**

(Individually Boxed)

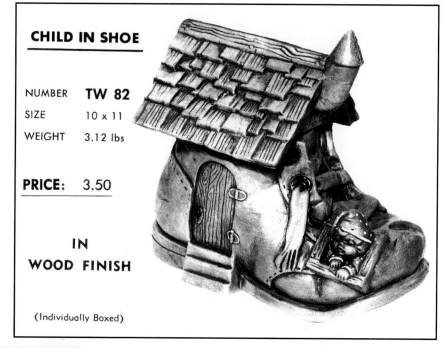

TW-82 Child In Shoe
Size: 10" x 11"
Weight: 3.12 lbs.
Colors: wf-i-g-a-p-o-r
Catalog(s): 1963, 1964, 1966, 1967, 1968, 1969, 1971, 1972, 1974, 1975
Value: $45.00

TW-45 Chipmunk
Size: 10" x 10"
Weight: 3.08 lbs.
Colors: wf-i-g-a-p-o-r
Catalog(s): 1964, 1966, 1967, 1968, 1969, 1971, 1972, 1974, 1975
Value: $75.00
Note: This is not a squirrel.

TW-52 Catcher
Size: 8" x 13"
Weight: 4.08 lbs.
Colors: wf-i-g-a-p-o-r
Catalog(s): 1961, 1963, 1964, 1966, 1967,
1968, 1969, 1971, 1972, 1974, 1975
Value: $100.00

TW-59 Cookie Bucket
Size: 8" x 9"
Weight: 3.02 lbs.
Colors: wf-i-g-a-p-o-r
Catalog(s): 1963, 1964, 1966, 1967
1968, 1969, 1971, 1972, 1974, 1975
Value: $40.00

TW-48 Cookie Cart
Size: 7" x 12"
Weight: 3.10 lbs.
Colors: wf-i-g-a-p-o-r
Catalog(s): 1969, 1971, 1972
Value: $125.00

TW-72 Cookie Churn
Size: 7" x 12"
Weight: 3.04 lbs.
Colors: wf-i-g-a-p-o-r
Catalog(s): 1963, 1964, 1966,
1967, 1968, 1969, 1971, 1972
Value: $125.00

TW-99 Cookie Coach
Size: 9" x 11"
Weight: 3.10 lbs.
Colors: wf-i-g-a-p-o-r
Catalog(s): 1972, 1974, 1975
Value: $200.00

TW-57 Cookie Elf
Size: 8½" x 12"
Weight: 4.00 lbs.
Colors: wf-i-g-a-p-o-r
Catalog(s): 1963, 1964, 1966, 1967, 1968,
1969, 1971, 1972, 1974, 1975
Value: $65.00
Note: Picture is green, catalog says wood
finish.

TW-96 Cookie Guard
Size: 7" x 12"
Weight: 4.00 lbs.
Colors: wf-i-g-a-p-o-r
Catalog(s): 1969
Value: $400.00

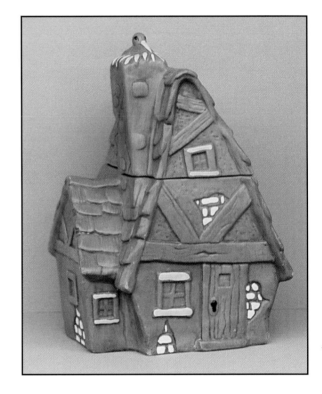

TW-83 Cookie Nut
Size: 9" x 10"
Weight: 3.02 lbs.
Colors: wf-i-g-a-p-o-r
Catalog(s): 1963, 1964, 1966,
1967, 1968, 1969, 1971, 1972
Value: $65.00

TW-97 Cookie Shack
Size: 9" x 12"
Weight: 3.10 lbs.
Colors: wf-i-g-a-p-o-r
Catalog(s): 1961, 1963, 1964, 1966, 1967,
1968, 1969, 1971, 1972, 1974, 1975
Value: $55.00

TW-96 Cookie Tepee
Size: 8" x 11"
Weight: 3.02 lbs.
Colors: wf
Catalog(s): 1961, 1963, 1964, 1966
Value: $325.00

TW-81 Cookie Time
Size: 7½" x 14"
Weight: 3.10 lbs.
Colors: wf-i-g-a-p-o-r
Catalog(s): 1963, 1964, 1966,
1967, 1968, 1969, 1971, 1972,
1974, 1975
Value: $45.00

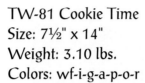

TW-49 Cop
Size: 7" x 12½"
Weight: 3.08 lbs.
Colors: wf-i-g-a-p-o-r
Catalog(s): 1964, 1966, 1967, 1968,
1969, 1971, 1972, 1974, 1975
Value: $100.00

TW-69 Cow
Size: 8½" x 13½"
Weight: 4.04 lbs.
Colors: wf-i-g-a-p-o-r
Catalog(s): 1963, 1964, 1966, 1967,
1968, 1969, 1971, 1972, 1974, 1975
Value: $75.00
(This has turned up in Alberta molds.)

TW-51 Dinosaur
Size: 8" x 13"
Weight: 4.02 lbs.
Colors: wf
Catalog(s): 1961, 1963, 1964, 1966, 1967, 1968
Value: $350.00

DOBBIN

NUMBER	**TW 80**	
SIZE	7 ½ x 14	
WEIGHT	4.02 lbs	

PRICE: 3.50

**IN
WOOD FINISH**

(Individually Boxed)

TW-71 Dog In Basket
Size: 8½" x 10"
Weight: 3.02 lbs.
Colors: wf-i-g-a-p-o-r
Catalog(s): 1963, 1964, 1966, 1967, 1968, 1969, 1971
Value: $85.00

TW-80 Dobbin
Size: 7½" x 14"
Weight: 4.02 lbs.
Colors: wf-i-g-a-p-o-r
Catalog(s): 1961, 1963, 1964, 1966, 1967, 1968, 1969, 1971, 1972, 1974, 1975
Value: $95.00

DOG ON DRUM

NUMBER **TW 93**

SIZE 7 x 12

WEIGHT 3.06 lbs

PRICE: 3.50

IN
WOOD FINISH

(Individually Boxed)

TW-93 Dog On Drum
Size: 7" x 12"
Weight: 3.06 lbs.
Colors: wf
Catalog(s): 1961, 1963,
1964, 1966, 1967, 1968
Value: $150.00

DUCK

NUMBER **TW 79**

SIZE 9 x 12

WEIGHT 3.08 lbs

PRICE: 3.50

IN
WOOD FINISH

(Individually Boxed)

TW-88 Donkey
Size: 8" x 13"
Weight: 3.06 lbs.
Colors: wf-i-g-a-p-o-r
Catalog(s): 1963, 1964, 1966,
1967, 1968, 1969, 1971, 1972,
1974, 1975
Value: $65.00

TW-79 Duck
Size: 9" x 12"
Weight: 3.08 lbs.
Colors: wf-i-g-a-p-o-r
Catalog(s): 1963, 1964, 1966,
1967, 1968, 1969, 1971
Value: $150.00

TW-93 Duckling
Size: 8" x 11"
Weight: 3.02 lbs.
Colors: wf-i-g-a-p-o-r
Catalog(s): 1971, 1972
Value: $250.00

TW-47 Dutch Girl
Size: 8½" x 12½"
Weight: 3.06 lbs.
Colors: wf-i-g-a-p-o-r
Catalog(s): 1963, 1964, 1966, 1967,
1968, 1969, 1971, 1972, 1974, 1975
Value: $100.00

TW-86 Elephant
Size: 9½" x 12"
Weight: 4.00 lbs.
Colors: wf-i-g-a-p-o-r
Catalog(s): 1963, 1964, 1966, 1967,
1968, 1969, 1971, 1972, 1974, 1975
Value: $40.00
Note: Common name is Sailor Elephant.

TW-56 Fire Engine
Size: 7" x 12"
Weight: 6.00 lbs.
Colors: wf-i-g-a-p-o-r
Catalog(s): 1963, 1964, 1966, 1967,
1968, 1969, 1971, 1972, 1974
Value: $85.00

FOO DOG

NUMBER	TW 51
SIZE	8 x 12
WEIGHT	3.08 lbs

PRICES

WOOD FINISH	3.50
IN COLOR (A-P-O-R)	4.00

(Individually Boxed)

TW-51 Foo Dog
Size: 8" x 12"
Weight: 3.08 lbs.
Colors: wf-i-g-a-p-o-r
Catalog(s): 1971
Value: $400.00

TW-50 Elf Bakery
Size: 8¾" x 12"
Weight: 3.08 lbs.
Colors: wf-i-g-a-p-o-r
Catalog(s): 1963, 1964, 1966, 1967,
1968, 1969, 1971, 1972, 1974, 1975
Value: $90.00

TW-85 Friar Tuck
Size: 7" x 12"
Weight: 3.08 lbs.
Colors: wf-i-g-a-p-o-r
Catalog(s): 1963, 1964,
1966, 1967, 1968, 1969,
1971, 1972, 1974, 1975
Value: $65.00

TW-73 Frog
Size: 8" x 9"
Weight: 3.02 lbs.
Colors: wf
Catalog(s): 1963, 1964, 1966
Value: $350.00

TW-75 Goose
Size: 7" x 14"
Weight: 3.10 lbs.
Colors: wf-i-g-a-p-o-r
Catalog(s): 1961, 1963, 1964,
1966, 1967, 1968, 1969,
1971, 1972, 1974, 1975
Value: $100.00
Note: Common name is
Mother Goose.

TW-39 Gorilla
Size: 8" x 12"
Weight: 3.00 lbs.
Colors: wf-i-g-a-p-o-r
Catalog(s): 1968, 1969
Value: $350.00
Note: Common name
is Magilla Gorilla.

TW-58 Grandma
Size: 7" x 10"
Weight: 3.08 lbs.
Colors: wf
Catalog(s): 1963, 1964, 1966
Value: $250.00

TW-95 Happy Bull
Size: 8½" x 12"
Weight: 3.08 lbs.
Colors: wf-i-g-a-p-o-r
Catalog(s): 1961, 1963, 1964, 1966, 1967,
1968, 1969, 1971, 1972, 1974, 1975
Value: $85.00
Note: In 1961 it was called Ferdinand, in
1963 and after called Happy Bull.

TW-61 Hen On Basket
Size: 8½" x 8½"
Weight: 3.04 lbs.
Colors: wf-i-g-a-p-o-r
Catalog(s): 1964, 1966, 1967, 1968, 1969
Value: $125.00

HIPPO

NUMBER	**TW 67**
SIZE	7 x 11
WEIGHT	3.08 lbs

PRICE: 3.50

**IN
WOOD FINISH
ONLY**

(Individually Boxed)

TW-67 Hippo
Size: 7" x 11"
Weight: 3.08 lbs.
Colors: wf-i-g-a-p-o-r
Catalog(s): 1969
Value: $400.00

HOTEI

NUMBER	**TW 78**
SIZE	9 x 12½
WEIGHT	4.00 lbs

PRICE: 3.50

**IN
WOOD FINISH**

(Individually Boxed)

TW-78 Hotei
Size: 9" x 12½"
Weight: 4.00 lbs.
Colors: wf-i-g-a-p-o-r
Catalog(s): 1963, 1964, 1966,
1967, 1968, 1969, 1971,
1972, 1974, 1975
Value: $65.00

TW-40 House
Size: 8" x 12"
Colors: wf
Catalog(s): 1967, 1968
Value: $175.00

TW-48 Jack In The Box
Size: 10" x 13½"
Weight: 4.10 lbs.
Colors: wf
Catalog(s): 1963, 1964, 1966
Value: $350.00

TW-99 Kangaroo
Size: 7½" x 13"
Weight: 3.08 lbs.
Colors: wf
Catalog(s): 1963, 1964, 1966, 1967, 1968
Value: $300.00

KITTEN IN BASKET

NUMBER	**TW 70**
SIZE	8½ x 10
WEIGHT	3.02 lbs

PRICE: 3.50

**IN
WOOD FINISH**

(Individually Boxed)

TW-70 Kitten In Basket
Size: 8½" x 10"
Weight: 3.02 lbs.
Colors: wf-i-g-a-p-o-r
Catalog(s): 1963, 1964, 1966, 1967, 1968, 1969, 1971
Value: $65.00

LIGHTHOUSE

NUMBER	**TW 42**
SIZE	7 x 13
WEIGHT	3.02 lbs.

PRICE: 3.50

**IN
WOOD FINISH**

(Individually Boxed)

TW-90 Lion
Size: 7" x 13"
Weight: 3.12 lbs.
Colors: wf-i-g-a-p-o-r
Catalog(s): 1963, 1964, 1966, 1967, 1968, 1969, 1971, 1972, 1974, 1975
Value: $50.00

TW-42 Lighthouse
Size: 7" x 13"
Weight: 3.02 lbs.
Colors: wf
Catalog(s): 1968
Value: $400.00

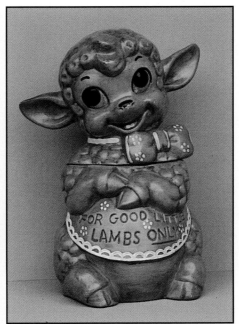

TW-66 Little Lamb
Size: 8" x 13"
Weight: 3.04 lbs.
Colors: wf-i-g-a-p-o-r
Catalog(s): 1963, 1964, 1966, 1967, 1968, 1969, 1971, 1972, 1974, 1975
Value: $40.00
(This piece has shown up in Alberta molds.)

TW-98 Modern Head
Size: 8" x 13"
Weight: 3.10 lbs.
Colors: wf
Catalog(s): 1961, 1963, 1964
Value: $450.00

TW-63 Mouse
Size: 7" x 12"
Weight: 3.10 lbs.
Colors: wf-i-g-a-p-o-r
Catalog(s): 1969, 1971, 1972, 1974, 1975
Value: $75.00
Note: Common name is Sailor Mouse.

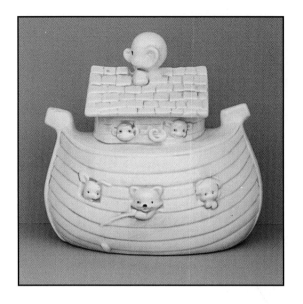

TW-94 Noah's Ark
Size: 9½" x 10"
Weight: 3.02 lbs.
Colors: wf-i-g-a-p-o-r
Catalog(s): 1963, 1964, 1966,
1967, 1968, 1969, 1971
Value: $75.00

TW-55 Ole King Cole
Size: 7" x 10"
Weight: 3.08 lbs.
Colors: wf
Catalog(s): 1963, 1964
Value: $400.00

TW-91 Owl
Size: 6½" x 12"
Weight: 3.04 lbs.
Colors: wf-i-g-a-p-o-r
Catalog(s): 1963, 1964, 1966, 1967,
1968, 1969, 1971, 1972, 1974, 1975
Value: $40.00

PEANUT MAN

NUMBER	**TW 55**
SIZE	8 x 13
WEIGHT	3.04 lbs.

PRICE: 3.50

**IN
WOOD FINISH**

(Individually Boxed)

TW-55 Peanut Man
Size: 8" x 13"
Weight: 3.04 lbs.
Colors: wf
Catalog(s): 1968
Value: $1,000.00
(None known to exist.)

PEAR

NUMBER	**TW 36**
SIZE	7 x 12
WEIGHT	3.04 lbs

PRICES

WOOD FINISH 3.50

**IN COLOR
(A-P-O-R)** 4.00

(Individually Boxed)

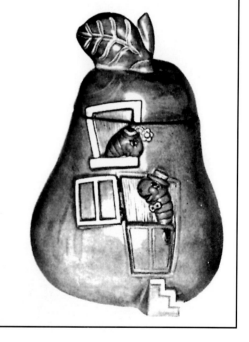

TW-46 Pirate Fox
Size: 8½" x 11"
Weight: 3.08 lbs.
Colors: wf-i-g-a-p-o-r
Catalog(s): 1964, 1966, 1967, 1968,
1969, 1971, 1972, 1974, 1975
Value: $85.00

TW-36 Pear
Size: 7" x 12"
Weight: 3.04 lbs.
Colors: wf-i-g-a-p-o-r
Catalog(s): 1971, 1972
Value: $120.00

TW-44 Persian Kitten
Size: 8" x 12"
Weight: 4.02 lbs.
Colors: wf-i-g-a-p-o-r
Catalog(s): 1964, 1966, 1967, 1968,
1969, 1971, 1972, 1974, 1975
Value: $140.00

TW-64 Poodle
Size: 7½" x 13"
Weight: 3.08 lbs.
Colors: wf-i-g-a-p-o-r
Catalog(s): 1964, 1966, 1967, 1968,
1969, 1971, 1972, 1974, 1975
Value: $85.00

W-76 Porky Pig
Size: 7½" x 12"
Weight: 3.06 lbs.
Colors: wf-i-g-a-p-o-r
Catalog(s): 1963, 1964, 1966,
1967, 1968, 1969, 1971, 1972,
1974, 1975
Value: $100.00

TW-38 Pot Bellied Stove
Size: 7" x 12"
Weight: 3.06 lbs.
Colors: wf-i-g-a-p-o-r
Catalog(s): 1969, 1971, 1972,
1974, 1975
Value: $85.00

TW-87 Rabbit
Size: 8" x 13"
Weight: 3.04 lbs.
Colors: wf-i-g-a-p-o-r
Catalog(s): 1963, 1964, 1966, 1967,
1968, 1969, 1971, 1972, 1974,
1975
Value: $75.00
Note: Common name is Gunfighter
Rabbit.

TW-58 Pot O'Cookies
Size: 8" x 10"
Weight: 4.00 lbs.
Colors: wf-i-g-a-p-o-r
Catalog(s): 1969, 1971,
1972, 1974, 1975
Value: $40.00

ROOSTER

NUMBER **TW 68**
SIZE 10 x 12
WEIGHT 3.10 lbs

PRICE: 3.50

**IN
WOOD FINISH**

(Individually Boxed)

TW-92 Raccoon
Size: 8" x 11½"
Weight: 3.10 lbs.
Colors: wf-i-g-a-p-o-r
Catalog(s): 1963, 1964, 1966, 1967,
1968, 1969, 1971, 1972, 1974, 1975
Value: $50.00

TW-68 Rooster
Size: 10" x 12"
Weight: 3.10 lbs.
Colors: wf-i-g-a-p-o-r
Catalog(s): 1963, 1964, 1966, 1967,
1968, 1969, 1971, 1972, 1974, 1975
Value: $75.00

TW-40 Shaggy Pup
Size: 8" x 11"
Weight: 4.00 lbs.
Colors: wf-i-g-a-p-o-r
Catalog(s): 1974
Value: $300.00

SHAGGY PUP

CODE NUMBERS

40-W
(Wood Finish)

40-G
(Gray Finish)

PRICE: 4.50

SIZE 8 x 11
WEIGHT 4.00 lbs

(Individually Boxed)

TW-55 Sheriff
Size: 8" x 11"
Weight: 3.08 lbs.
Colors: wf-i-g-a-p-o-r
Catalog(s): 1971, 1972, 1974, 1975
Value: $75.00

TW-37 Snail
Size: 7½" x 12"
Weight: 3.08 lbs.
Colors: wf-i-g-a-p-o-r
Catalog(s): 1969, 1971, 1972
Value: $175.00

TW-74 Squirrel
Size: 6" x 10½"
Weight: 3.02 lbs.
Colors: wf-i-g-a-p-o-r
Catalog(s): 1963, 1964, 1966, 1967,
1968, 1969, 1971, 1972, 1974, 1975
Value: $45.00

TW-65 Stove
Size: 8" x 13"
Weight: 4.16 lbs.
Colors: wf-i-g-a-p-o-r
Catalog(s): 1966, 1967, 1968,
1969, 1971, 1972, 1974, 1975
Value: $75.00

TW-53 Teddy Bear
Size: 8" x 10"
Weight: 3.02 lbs.
Colors: wf-i-g-a-p-o-r
Catalog(s): 1963, 1964, 1966, 1967,
1968, 1969, 1971, 1972, 1974, 1975
Value: $85.00

TOMMY TURTLE

NUMBER	**TW 77**
SIZE	13 x 8
WEIGHT	3.06 lbs

PRICE: 3.50

IN
WOOD FINISH

(Individually Boxed)

TW-77 Tommy Turtle
Size: 13" x 8"
Weight: 3.06 lbs.
Colors: wf-i-g-a-p-o-r
Catalog(s): 1963, 1964, 1966, 1967,
1968, 1969, 1971, 1972, 1974, 1975
Value: $125.00

TW-89 Train
Size: 7" x 13"
Weight: 3.00 lbs.
Colors: wf-i-g-a-p-o-r
Catalog(s): 1963, 1964, 1966, 1967,
1968, 1969, 1971, 1972, 1974, 1975
Value: $75.00

TW-63 Walrus
Size: 10" x 11"
Weight: 3.06 lbs.
Colors: wf
Catalog(s): 1964, 1966
Value: $375.00

TW-43 Tug
Size: 7" x 12"
Weight: 3.02 lbs.
Colors: wf-i-g-a-p-o-r
Catalog(s): 1968, 1969
Value: $350.00

TW-62 Wheel Barrow
Size: 8" x 10"
Weight: 3.04 lbs.
Colors: wf-i-g-a-p-o-r
Catalog(s): 1971
Value: $400.00

COLLECTOR SERIES COOKIE JARS

The Collector Series of cookie jars was introduced in 1974 and was produced until the company was sold in 1976. There were only 18 designs produced in this decorating method according to the catalogs. I have seen some salt and pepper sets as well as other items that were produced with the same decorating color themes. Some of the employees made gifts for friends and family as well as special custom orders by the salesmen. Therefore, you may find anything in the line in this same color theme.

Front cover of the Collector Series section of the 1974 catalog.

Dealer plaque
Value: $450.00

    I cannot confirm the author of the following, however, I believe it to be Bruce Winton. Whoever wrote this (found in the 1974 catalog) certainly had an insight into the future. With the year 2000 approaching rapidly we have all seen the value of these wonderful pieces climb dramatically. Perhaps, by the year 2074, what the author wrote will be true and we will all be amazed at the value of these delightful creations designed by Don Winton.

Back page of the Collector Series section of the 1974 catalog, entitled "Nostalgia."

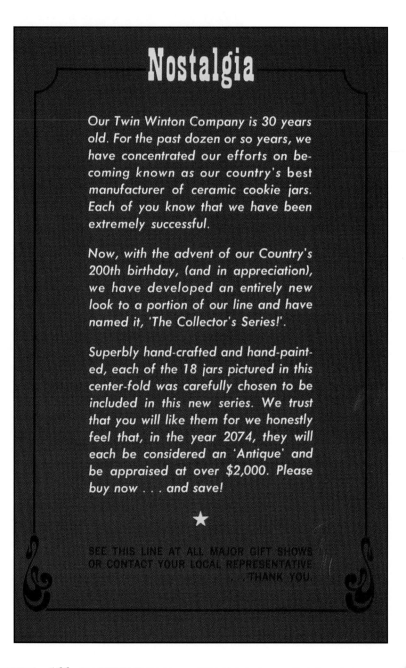

Nostalgia

Our Twin Winton Company is 30 years old. For the past dozen or so years, we have concentrated our efforts on becoming known as our country's best manufacturer of ceramic cookie jars. Each of you know that we have been extremely successful.

Now, with the advent of our Country's 200th birthday, (and in appreciation), we have developed an entirely new look to a portion of our line and have named it, 'The Collector's Series!'.

Superbly hand-crafted and hand-painted, each of the 18 jars pictured in this center-fold was carefully chosen to be included in this new series. We trust that you will like them for we honestly feel that, in the year 2074, they will each be considered an 'Antique' and be appraised at over $2,000. Please buy now . . . and save!

★

SEE THIS LINE AT ALL MAJOR GIFT SHOWS
OR CONTACT YOUR LOCAL REPRESENTATIVE
. . . THANK YOU.

Page one of the Collector Series section of the 1974 catalog.

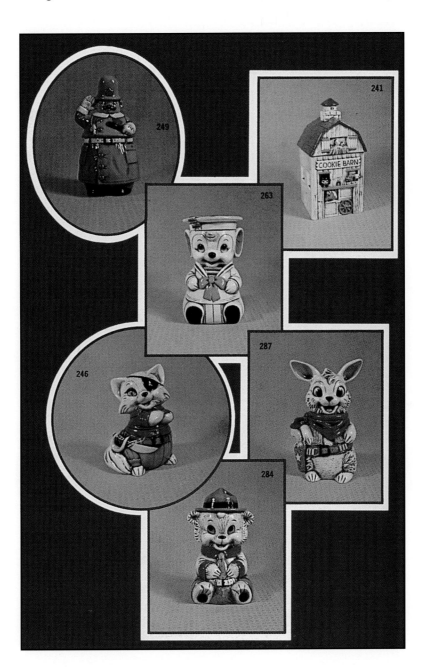

Stock #	Title	Value
TW-249	Policeman (Cop)	$225.00
TW-241	Cookie Barn	$175.00
TW-263	Mouse	$225.00
TW-246	Pirate Fox	$225.00
TW-287	Rabbit	$200.00
TW284	Bear	$125.00

Page two of the Collector Series section of the 1974 catalog.

Stock #	Title	Value
TW-243	Flopsy	$350.00
TW-242	Mopsy	$350.00
TW-286	Elephant	$125.00
TW-247	Dutch Girl	$225.00
TW-288	Donkey	$175.00
TW291	Owl	$125.00

Page three of the Collector Series section of the 1974 catalog.

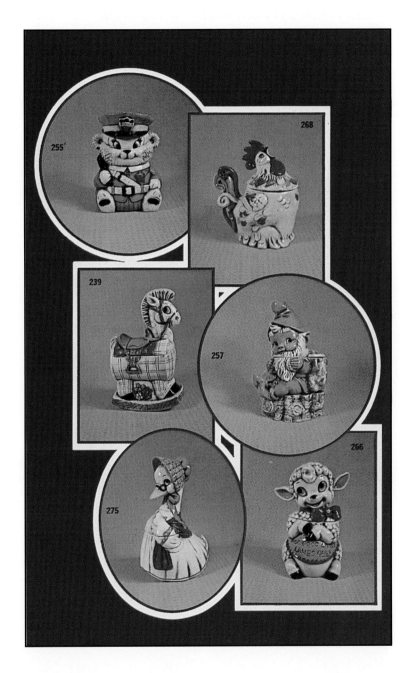

Stock #	Title	Value
TW-255	Sheriff	$200.00
TW-268	Rooster	$175.00
TW-239	Hobby Horse	$300.00
TW-257	Cookie Elf	$225.00
TW-275	Goose	$275.00
TW-266	Lamb	$175.00

Don't you wish you could still purchase these pieces for only $7.50 each! It is important to note, according to the catalogs, that three of the pieces were only offered in the Collector Series and not in the wood stain.

Page four of the Collector Series section of the 1974 catalog.

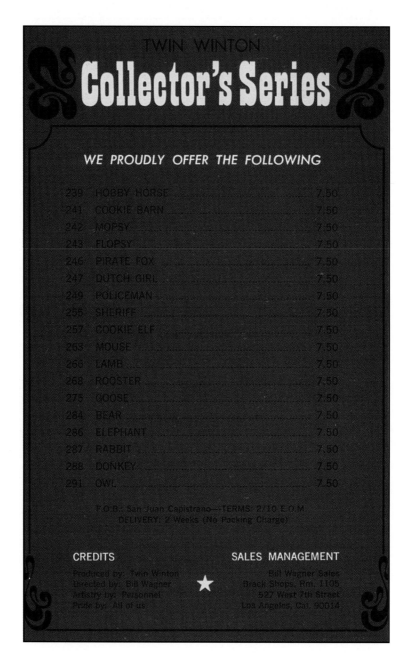

Stock #	Title		Value
TW-239	Hobby Horse	Collectors Series Only	$300.00
TW-242	Mopsy	Collectors Series Only	$350.00
TW-243	Flopsy	Collectors Series Only	$350.00

(These three were offered only in the 1974 & 1975 catalog collector series.)

TW-284 Bear
Size: 7" x 12"
Colors: cs
Catalog(s): 1974, 1975
Value: $125.00
Note: Common name is Ranger Bear. (This series did not have one with a badge.)

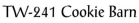

TW-241 Cookie Barn
Size: 8" x 12"
Colors: cs
Catalog(s): 1974, 1975
Value: $175.00

TW-257 Cookie Elf
Size: 8½" x 12"
Colors: cs
Catalog(s): 1974, 1975
Value: $225.00

TW-243 Flopsy
Size: 7" x 12"
Colors: cs
Catalog(s): 1974, 1975
Value: $350.00
Note: Introduced in 1974 for the collector series. This was not listed in a previous catalog. Common name is Raggedy Andy. (Very few if any were offered in the wood stain finish.)

TW-288 Donkey
Size: 8" x 13"
Colors: cs
Catalog(s): 1974, 1975
Value: $175.00

TW-247 Dutch Girl
Size: 8½" x 12"
Colors: cs
Catalog(s): 1974, 1975
Value: $225.00

ELEPHANT

CODE NUMBERS

86-W
(Wood Finish)

86-G
(Gray Finish)

PRICE: 4.50

SIZE   9½ x 12

WEIGHT   4.00 lbs

(Individually Boxed)

TW-286 Elephant
Size: 9½" x 12"
Colors: cs
Catalog(s): 1974, 1975
Value: $300.00
Note: Common name is Sailor
Elephant. (Very few if any
offered in the wood stain finish.)

TW-275 Goose
Size: 7" x 14"
Colors: cs
Catalog(s): 1974, 1975
Value: $275.00
Note: Common name is Mother Goose.

TW-242 Mopsy
Size: 7" x 12"
Colors: cs
Catalog(s): 1974, 1975
Value: $350.00
Note: Introduced in 1974 for the col-
lector series. This was not listed in a
previous catalog. Common name is
Raggedy Ann. (Very few if any were
offered in the wood stain finish.)

TW-239 Hobby Horse
Size: 8½" x 12"
Colors: cs
Catalog(s): 1974, 1975
Value: $300.00
Note: Introduced in 1974 for the collector series. This was not listed in a previous catalog. (Very few if any were offered in the wood stain finish.)

LITTLE LAMB

NUMBER	**TW 66**
SIZE	8 x 13
WEIGHT	3.04 lbs

PRICE: 3.50

IN
WOOD FINISH

(Individually Boxed)

TW-266 Lamb
Size: 8" x 13"
Colors: cs
Catalog(s): 1974, 1975
Value: $175.00

TW-263 Mouse
Size: 7" x 12"
Colors: cs
Catalog(s): 1974, 1975
Value: $225.00
Note: Common name is Sailor Mouse

TW-291 Owl
Size: 6½" x 12"
Colors: cs
Catalog(s): 1974, 1975
Value: $125.00

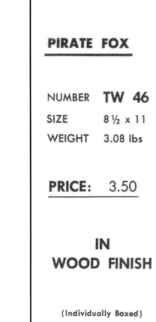

PIRATE FOX

NUMBER	**TW 46**
SIZE	8 ½ x 11
WEIGHT	3.08 lbs

PRICE: 3.50

**IN
WOOD FINISH**

(Individually Boxed)

TW-246 Pirate Fox
Size: 8½" x 11"
Colors: cs
Catalog(s): 1974, 1975
Value: $225.00

TW-249 Policeman (Cop)
Size: 7" x 12½"
Colors: cs
Catalog(s): 1974, 1975
Value: $225.00

TW-287 Rabbit
Size: 8" x 13"
Colors: cs
Catalog(s): 1974, 1975
Value: $200.00
Note: Common name is Gunfighter Rabbit.

ROOSTER

CODE NUMBERS

68-W
(Wood Finish)

68-G
(Gray Finish)

PRICE: 4.50

SIZE   10 x 12
WEIGHT   3.10 lbs

(Individually Boxed)

TW-268 Rooster
Size: 10" x 12"
Colors: cs
Catalog(s): 1974, 1975
Value: $125.00

TW-255 Sheriff
Size: 8" x 11"
Colors: cs
Catalog(s): 1974, 1975
Value: $200.00

SALT & PEPPER SHAKERS

The salt and pepper shakers appear to have been part of the line from a very early stage of the business. In 1947, after the boys returned from the war, they were making Hillbilly shakers. Early animal shakers have also appeared. The ones listed in this chapter are those specifically listed in the Twin Winton catalogs. The decorating of these wonderful designs will also vary along the same lines as the cookie jars. Don said that he once turned out over 60 designs of salt and pepper shakers for one company. The designs that are not mentioned here will have to be shown in a different book.

Information from the catalog years 1962, 1965, and 1973 was not available at time of printing.

Key to colors:

wf: wood finish	i: ivory	g: gray	a: avocado
p: pineapple	o: orange	r: red	

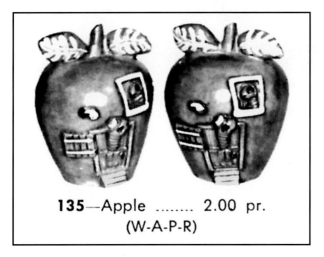

135—Apple .... 2.00 pr.
(W-A-P-R)

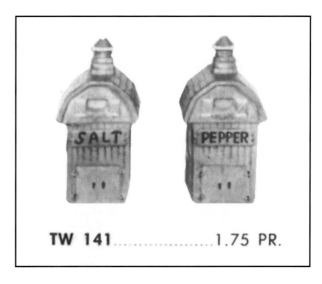

TW 141 .... 1.75 PR.

TW-135 Apple
Colors: wf-g-i-a-p-o-r
Catalog(s): 1971, 1972
Value: $75.00

TW-141 Barn
Colors: wf-g-i-a-p-o-r
Catalog(s): 1967, 1968, 1969, 1971, 1972, 1974, 1975
Value: $40.00
Note: Also listed under canisters.

TW 162 Barrel..........1.75 pr.

TW-162 Barrel
Colors: wf-g-i-a-p-o-r
Catalog(s): 1964, 1966, 1967, 1968
Value: $50.00
Note: There is a later version of this with the mouse finial.

TW-184 Bear
Colors: wf-g-i-a-p-o-r
Catalog(s): 1963, 1964, 1966, 1967, 1968, 1969, 1971, 1972, 1974, 1975
Value: $40.00
Note: Common name is Ranger Bear.

TW-195 Bull
Colors: wf-g-i-a-p-o-r
Catalog(s): 1961, 1963, 1964, 1966, 1967, 1968, 1969, 1972, 1974, 1975
Value: $40.00
Note: In a 1961 flier this was listed as Ferdinand the Bull. It was changed to Happy Bull in 1963 catalog.

TW-65 Bucket
Colors: wf-g-i-a-p-o-r
Catalog(s): 1963
Value: $30.00
Note: Changed to stock #159 in 1964.

TW-159 Bucket
Colors: wf-g-i-a-p-o-r
Catalog(s): 1964, 1966, 1967, 1968,
1969, 1971, 1972, 1974, 1975
Value: $30.00
Note: Changed from stock #65.

TW 160 Butler..........1.75 pr.

198—Cable Car   **2.25 pr.**

TW-160 Butler
Colors: wf-g-i-a-p-o-r
Catalog(s): 1964, 1966,
1967, 1968, 1969
Value: $50.00

TW-198 Cable Car
Colors: wf-g-i-a-p-o-r
Catalog(s): 1971, 1972, 1974, 1975
Value: $50.00

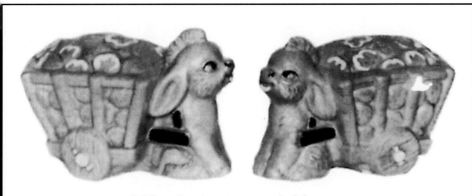

148—Cart .... 2.00 pr.
(W-G-A-P-O)

TW-148 Cart
Colors: wf-g-i-a-p-o-r
Catalog(s): 1971, 1972, 1974
Value: $50.00

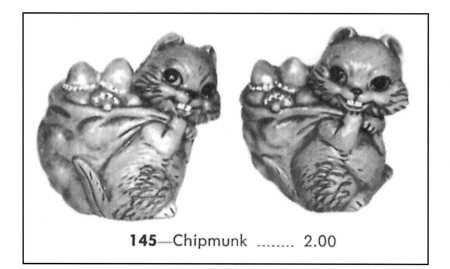

145—Chipmunk 2.00

TW-145 Chipmunk
Colors: wf-g-i-a-p-o-r
Catalog(s): 1964, 1966, 1967, 1968,
1969, 1971, 1972, 1974, 1975
Value: $40.00

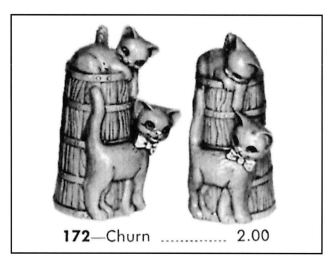

172—Churn 2.00

TW-172 Churn
Colors: wf-g-i-a-p-o-r
Catalog(s): 1963, 1964, 1966, 1967,
1968, 1969, 1971, 1972, 1974
Value: $40.00

158—Cookie Pot   2.25 pr.

TW-158 Cookie Pot
Colors: wf-g-i-a-p-o-r
Catalog(s): 1969, 1971, 1972, 1974, 1975
Value: $30.00

TW-149 Cop
Colors: wf-g-i-a-p-o-r
Catalog(s): 1964, 1966, 1967, 1968,
1969, 1971, 1972, 1974, 1975
Value: $40.00

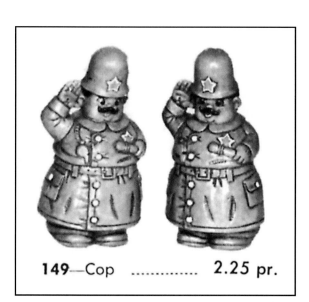

149—Cop   .... 2.25 pr.

TW-169 Cow
Colors: wf-g-i-a-p-o-r
Catalog(s): 1963, 1964, 1966, 1967, 1968, 1969, 1971, 1972, 1974, 1975
Value: $50.00

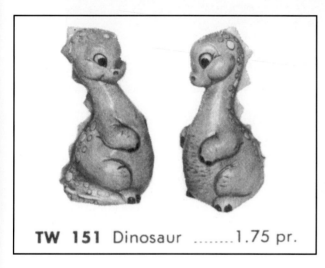

TW 151 Dinosaur ....1.75 pr.

TW 180 Dobbin ....1.75 pr.

TW-151 Dinosaur
Colors: wf-g-i-a-p-o-r
Catalog(s): 1961, 1963, 1964, 1966, 1967, 1968
Value: $100.00

TW-180 Dobbin
Colors: wf-g-i-a-p-o-r
Catalog(s): 1961, 1963, 1964, 1966, 1967, 1968, 1969, 1971, 1972, 1974, 1975
Value: $45.00

TW 171—Dog ....1.75 pr.

TW-171 Dog
Colors: wf-g-i-a-p-o-r
Catalog(s): 1963, 1964, 1966, 1967, 1968, 1969, 1971
Value: $40.00

TW-188 Donkey
Colors: wf-g-i-a-p-o-r
Catalog(s): 1963, 1964, 1966, 1967,
1968, 1969, 1971, 1972, 1974, 1975
Value: $40.00

TW-179 Duck
Colors: wf-g-i-a-p-o-r
Catalog(s): 1963, 1964, 1966, 1967, 1968
Value: $75.00

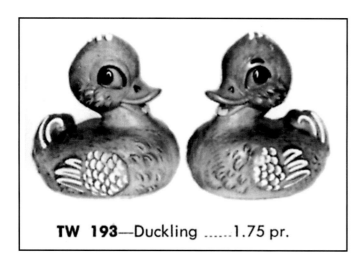

TW 193—Duckling ......1.75 pr.

TW-193 Duckling
Colors: wf-g-i-a-p-o-r
Catalog(s): 1971, 1972
Value: $75.00

TW-147 Dutch Girl
Colors: wf-g-i-a-p-o-r
Catalog(s): 1963, 1964, 1966, 1967,
1968, 1969, 1971, 1972, 1974, 1975
Value: $35.00

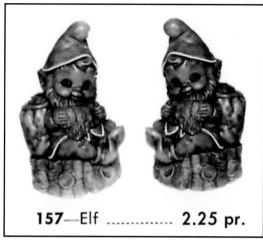

157—Elf .... 2.25 pr.

TW-157 Elf
Colors: wf-g-i-a-p-o-r
Catalog(s): 1963, 1964, 1966, 1967,
1968, 1969, 1971, 1972, 1974, 1975
Value: $40.00

TW-186 Elephant
Colors: wf-g-i-a-p-o-r
Catalog(s): 1963, 1964, 1966, 1967,
1968, 1969, 1971, 1972, 1974, 1975
Value: $35.00
Note: Common name is Sailor Elephant.

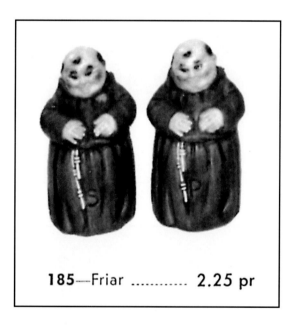

185—Friar .... 2.25 pr

TW-151 Foo Dog
Colors: wf-g-i-a-p-o-r
Catalog(s): 1971
Value: $125.00

TW-185 Friar
Colors: wf-g-i-a-p-o-r
Catalog(s): 1963, 1964, 1966, 1967, 1968, 1969,
1971, 1972, 1974, 1975
Value: $35.00
Note: Common name is Monk or Friar Tuck.

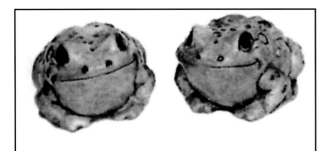

TW 173 Frog . . . . 1.50 pr.

TW-173 Frog
Colors: wf-g-i-a-p-o-r
Catalog(s): 1963, 1964
Value: $125.00

TW 175 Goose ....1.75 pr.

TW-175 Goose
Colors: wf-g-i-a-p-o-r
Catalog(s): 1963, 1964, 1966, 1967,
1968, 1969, 1971, 1972, 1974, 1975
Value: $45.00
Note: Common name is Mother Goose.

TW 161 Hen ....1.75 pr.

TW-161 Hen
Colors: wf-g-i-a-p-o-r
Catalog(s): 1964, 1966, 1967, 1968, 1969
Value: $50.00

TW-178 Hotei
Colors: wf-g-i-a-p-o-r
Catalog(s): 1963, 1964, 1966, 1967,
1968, 1969, 1971, 1972, 1974, 1975
Value: $30.00

TW 140 .... 1.75 PR.

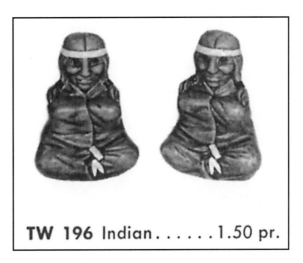

TW 196 Indian...... 1.50 pr.

TW-140 House
Colors: wf-g-i-a-p-o-r
Catalog(s): 1967, 1968
Value: $75.00
Note: Also listed under canisters.

TW-196 Indian (Chief)
Colors: wf-g-i-a-p-o-r
Catalog(s): 1961, 1963, 1964, 1966
Value: $75.00

TW 148 Jack in the Box 1.50 pr.

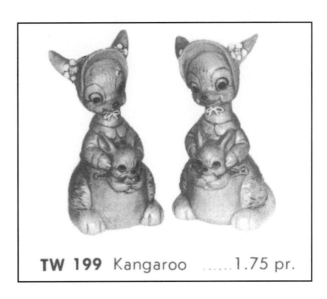

TW 199 Kangaroo ......1.75 pr.

TW-148 Jack In The Box
Colors: wf-g-i-a-p-o-r
Catalog(s): 1963, 1964
Value: $125.00

TW-199 Kangaroo
Colors: wf-g-i-a-p-o-r
Catalog(s): 1963, 1964,
1966, 1967, 1968
Value: $85.00

TW 144 Kitten .... 1.75 pr.

TW 170 Kitten .... 1.75 pr.

TW-144 Kitten (Persian)
Colors: wf-g-i-a-p-o-r
Catalog(s): 1964, 1966, 1967, 1968,
1969, 1971, 1972, 1974, 1975
Value: $40.00

TW-170 Kitten
Colors: wf-g-i-a-p-o-r
Catalog(s): 1963, 1964, 1966,
1967, 1968, 1969, 1971
Value: $40.00

TW-166 Lamb
Colors: wf-g-i-a-p-o-r
Catalog(s): 1963, 1964, 1966, 1967,
1968, 1969, 1971, 1972, 1974, 1975
Value: $30.00

TW-190 Lion
Colors: wf-g-i-a-p-o-r
Catalog(s): 1963, 1964, 1966, 1967,
1968, 1969, 1971, 1972, 1974, 1975
Value: $45.00

TW-163 Mouse
Colors: wf-g-i-a-p-o-r
Catalog(s): 1974, 1975
Value: $40.00
Note: Common name is Sailor Mouse.

TW-181 Mouse
Colors: wf-g-i-a-p-o-r
Catalog(s): 1963, 1964, 1966, 1967,
1968, 1969, 1971, 1972, 1974, 1975
Value: $40.00

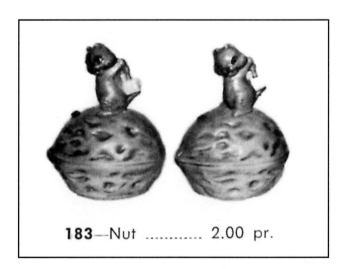

183—Nut .... 2.00 pr.

191—Owl .... 2.00 pr.
(W-G-A-P-O)

TW-183 Nut
Colors: wf-g-i-a-p-o-r
Catalog(s): 1971, 1972, 1974
Value: $75.00

TW-191 Owl
Colors: wf-g-i-a-p-o-r
Catalog(s): 1963, 1964, 1966, 1967,
1968, 1969, 1971, 1972, 1974, 1975
Value: $30.00

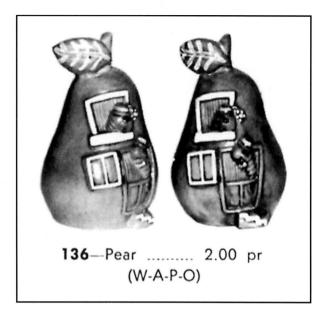

136—Pear .... 2.00 pr
(W-A-P-O)

TW-136 Pear
Colors: wf-g-i-a-p-o-r
Catalog(s): 1971, 1972
Value: $75.00

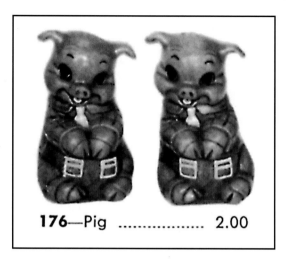

176—Pig 2.00

TW-176 Pig
Colors: wf-g-i-a-p-o-r
Catalog(s): 1963, 1964, 1966, 1967,
1968, 1969, 1971, 1972, 1974, 1975
Value: $50.00
Note: Common name is Porky Pig.

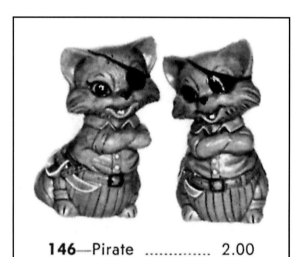

146—Pirate 2.00

TW-146 Pirate
Colors: wf-g-i-a-p-o-r
Catalog(s): 1964, 1966, 1967, 1968,
1969, 1971, 1972, 1974, 1975
Value: $45.00
Note: Common name is Pirate Fox.

TW-164 Poodle
Colors: wf-g-i-a-p-o-r
Catalog(s): 1966, 1967, 1968,
1969, 1971, 1972, 1974, 1975
Value: $50.00

164—Poodle .... 2.00 pr.

TW-138 Pot Bellied Stove
Colors: wf-g-i-a-p-o-r
Catalog(s): 1969, 1971, 1972, 1974, 1975
Value: $40.00

TW-187 Rabbit
Colors: wf-g-i-a-p-o-r
Catalog(s): 1963, 1964, 1966, 1967, 1968, 1969, 1971, 1972, 1974, 1975
Value: $45.00
Note: Common name is Gunfighter Rabbit.

TW-168 Rooster
Colors: wf-g-i-a-p-o-r
Catalog(s): 1963, 1964, 1966, 1967, 1968, 1969, 1971, 1972, 1974, 1975
Value: $30.00

TW-192 Raccoon
Colors: wf-g-i-a-p-o-r
Catalog(s): 1963, 1964, 1966, 1967, 1968, 1969, 1971, 1972, 1974, 1975
Value: $45.00

197—Shack .... 2.25 pr.

TW-197 Shack
Colors: wf-g-i-a-p-o-r
Catalog(s): 1971, 1972, 1974, 1975
Value: $40.00

TW-155 Sheriff
Colors: wf-g-i-a-p-o-r
Catalog(s): 1974, 1975
Value: $50.00

155 — Sheriff .... 2.25 pr.

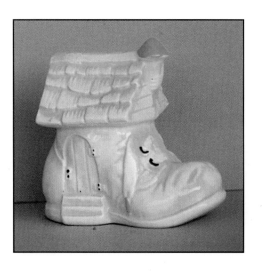

137—Snail .... 2.00 pr.

TW-182 Shoe
Colors: wf-g-i-a-p-o-r
Catalog(s): 1971, 1972, 1974, 1975
Value: $50.00

TW-137 Snail
Colors: wf-g-i-a-p-o-r
Catalog(s): 1972
Value: $125.00

174—Squirrel 2.00

153—Teddy Bear 2.00

TW-174 Squirrel
Colors: wf-g-i-a-p-o-r
Catalog(s): 1963, 1964, 1966, 1967,
1968, 1969, 1971, 1972, 1974, 1975
Value: $40.00

TW-153 Teddy Bear
Colors: wf-g-i-a-p-o-r
Catalog(s): 1966, 1967, 1968,
1969, 1971, 1972, 1974, 1975
Value: $50.00

165—Stove .... 2.25 pr.

TW-165 Stove
Colors: wf-g-i-a-p-o-r
Catalog(s): 1969, 1971,
1972, 1974, 1975
Value: $50.00

TW-177 Turtle
Colors: wf-g-i-a-p-o-r
Catalog(s): 1963, 1964, 1966, 1967,
1968, 1969, 1971, 1972, 1974, 1975
Value: $40.00
Note: Common name is Tommy Turtle.

177—Turtle .... 2.25 pr.

MISCELLANEOUS

This chapter deals with a variety of merchandise from ashtrays to wall planters. Some of these items only showed up in one catalog as an attempt to expand the line. Some of them were in all the catalogs and were consistent add-on sales. Whatever the case, you will find a treasure trove of designs that will delight you, the collector. Again the decorating of these items is similar to the decorating as listed in the chapter on Twin Winton cookie jars.

ASHTRAYS

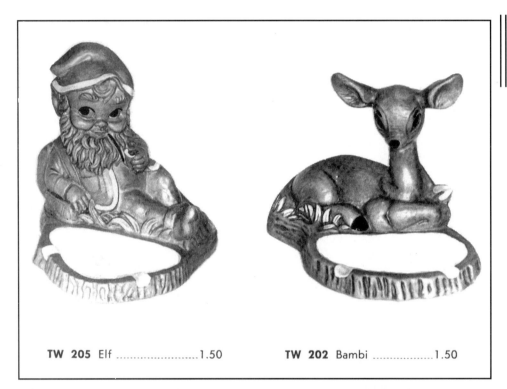

Key to colors:
wf: wood finish, i: ivory,
g: gray, a: avocado,
p: pineapple, o: orange, r: red.

TW 205 Elf .... 1.50 **TW 202** Bambi 1.50

TW-205 Elf
Item: Ashtray
Size: 8" x 8"
Colors: wf
Catalog(s): 1967, 1968
Value: $100.00

TW-202 Bambi
Item: Ashtray
Size: 6" x 8"
Colors: wf
Catalog(s): 1967, 1968
Value: $100.00

TW-201 Kitten
Item: Ashtray
Size: 6" x 8"
Colors: wf
Catalog(s): 1967, 1968
Value: $100.00

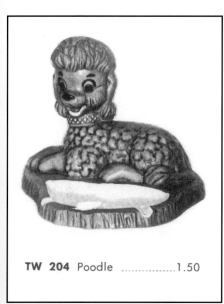

TW 204 Poodle 1.50

TW-204 Poodle
Item: Ashtray
Size: 6" x 8"
Colors: wf
Catalog(s): 1967, 1968
Value: $100.00

Bull
TW 413 ....1.50

TW-413 Bull
Item: Bank
Size: approx. 8" h
Colors: wf-i-g-a-p-o-r
Catalog(s): 1964, 1966, 1967, 1968, 1969, 1971, 1972, 1974, 1975
Value: $65.00

BANKS

TW-404 Bear
Item: Bank
Size: approx. 8" h
Colors: wf-i-g-a-p-o-r
Catalog(s): 1961, 1963, 1964, 1966, 1967, 1968, 1969, 1971, 1972, 1974, 1975
Value: $50.00
Note: Common name is Ranger Bear.

TW-412 Cop
Item: Bank
Size: approx. 8" h
Colors: wf-i-g-a-p-o-r
Catalog(s): 1964, 1966, 1967, 1968, 1969, 1971, 1972, 1974, 1975
Value: $65.00

Dobbin

TW 410 ....1.50

TW-410 Dobbin
Item: Bank
Size: approx. 8" h
Colors: wf-i-g-a-p-o-r
Catalog(s): 1963, 1964, 1966,
1967, 1968, 1969, 1971,
1972, 1974, 1975
Value: $40.00

TW-418 Dutch Girl
Item: Bank
Size: approx. 8" h
Colors: wf-i-g-a-p-o-r
Catalog(s): 1966, 1967, 1968,
1969, 1971, 1972, 1974, 1975
Value: $50.00

Dutch Girl

TW 418 ....1.50

TW-406 Elephant
Item: Bank
Size: approx. 8" h
Colors: wf-i-g-a-p-o-r
Catalog(s): 1961, 1963, 1964, 1966, 1967,
1968, 1969, 1971, 1972, 1974, 1975
Value: $50.00
Note: Common name
is Sailor Elephant.

TW-408 Elf
Item: Bank
Size: approx. 8" h
Colors: wf-i-g-a-p-o-r
Catalog(s): 1963, 1964,
1966, 1967, 1968, 1969,
1971, 1972, 1974, 1975
Value: $50.00

Elf

TW 408 ....1.50

Foo Dog Bank
TW 422 ....1.50

TW-422 Foo Dog
Item: Bank
Size: approx. 8" h
Colors: wf-i-g-a-p-o-r
Catalog(s): 1971
Value: $125.00

TW-407 Friar
Item: Bank
Size: approx. 8" h
Colors: wf-i-g-a-p-o-r
Catalog(s): 1963, 1964, 1966, 1967, 1968, 1969, 1971, 1972, 1974, 1975
Value: $40.00
Note: Common name is Monk or Friar Tuck.

Kitten
TW 415 ....1.50

TW-411 Hotei
Item: Bank
Size: approx. 8" h
Colors: wf-i-g-a-p-o-r
Catalog(s): 1963, 1964, 1966, 1967, 1968, 1969, 1971, 1972, 1974, 1975
Value: $50.00

TW-415 Kitten
Item: Bank
Size: approx. 8" h
Colors: wf-i-g-a-p-o-r
Catalog(s): 1964, 1966, 1967, 1968, 1969, 1971, 1972, 1974, 1975
Value: $50.00

TW-402 Lamb
Item: Bank
Size: approx. 8" h
Colors: wf-i-g-a-p-o-r
Catalog(s): 1961, 1963, 1964, 1966, 1967, 1968, 1969, 1971, 1972, 1974, 1975
Value: $40.00

TW-416 Nut
Item: Bank
Size: approx. 8" h
Colors: wf-i-g-a-p-o-r
Catalog(s): 1964, 1966, 1967, 1968, 1969, 1971, 1972, 1974, 1975
Value: $50.00

TW-420 Owl
Item: Bank
Size: approx. 8" h
Colors: wf-i-g-a-p-o-r
Catalog(s): 1969, 1971, 1972, 1974, 1975
Value: $65.00
Note: Not in 1969 catalog, but listed in memo.

TW-401 Pig
Item: Bank
Size: approx. 8" h
Colors: wf-i-g-a-p-o-r
Catalog(s): 1961, 1963, 1964, 1966, 1967,
1968, 1969, 1971, 1972, 1974, 1975
Value: $50.00

Pirate Fox
TW 414 ....1.50

TW-414 Pirate Fox
Item: Bank
Size: approx. 8" h
Colors: wf-i-g-a-p-o-r
Catalog(s): 1964, 1966, 1967, 1968,
1969, 1971, 1972, 1974, 1975
Value: $65.00

TW-419 Poodle
Item: Bank
Size: approx. 8" h
Colors: wf-i-g-a-p-o-r
Catalog(s): 1966, 1967, 1968,
1969, 1971, 1972, 1974, 1975
Value: $65.00

TW-405 Rabbit
Item: Bank
Size: approx. 8" h
Colors: wf-i-g-a-p-o-r
Catalog(s): 1961, 1963, 1964, 1966, 1967,
1968, 1969, 1971, 1972, 1974, 1975
Value: $50.00
Note: Common name is Gunfighter Rabbit.

Shack
TW 417 ....1.50

TW-417 Shack
Item: Bank
Size: approx. 8" h
Colors: wf-i-g-a-p-o-r
Catalog(s): 1964, 1966, 1967, 1968,
1969, 1971, 1972, 1974, 1975
Value: $50.00

Shoe Bank
TW 421 ....1.50

TW-421 Shoe
Item: Bank
Size: approx. 8" h
Colors: wf-i-g-a-p-o-r
Catalog(s): 1971, 1972, 1974, 1975
Value: $85.00

Squirrel

TW 403 ....1.50

TW-409 Teddy Bear
Item: Bank
Size: approx. 8" h
Colors: wf-i-g-a-p-o-r
Catalog(s): 1963, 1964, 1966, 1967,
1968, 1969, 1971, 1972, 1974, 1975
Value: $40.00

TW-403 Squirrel
Item: Bank
Size: approx. 8" h
Colors: wf-i-g-a-p-o-r
Catalog(s): 1963, 1964, 1966, 1967,
1968, 1969, 1971, 1972, 1974, 1975
Value: $40.00

CANDLEHOLDERS

TW-502L Strauss (Long)
Item: Candleholder
Size: 5" w x 10" h
Colors: wf-i-g-a-p-o-r
Catalog(s): 1972
Value: $15.00

TW-502S Strauss (Short)
Item: Candleholder
Size: 4½" w x 6" h
Colors: wf-i-g-a-p-o-r
Catalog(s): 1972
Value: $12.00

TW-501L Verdi (Long)
Item: Candleholder
Size: 4" w x 9½" h
Colors: wf-i-g-a-p-o-r
Catalog(s): 1972
Value: $15.00

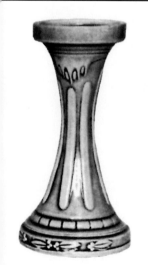

502L—Strauss 2.50
5" x 10"
(W-G-A-P-O-I)

502S—Strauss 1.75
4½" x 6"
(W-G-A-P-O-I)

501L—Verdi 2.50
4" x 9½"
(W-G-A-P-O-I)

503L—Ravel 2.50
5" x 9"
(W-G-A-P-O-I)

501S—Verdi 1.75
4" x 6"
(W-G-A-P-O-I)

TW-503L Ravel (Long)
Item: Candleholder
Size: 5" w x 9" h
Colors: wf-i-g-a-p-o-r
Catalog(s): 1972
Value: $18.00

TW-501S Verdi (Short)
Item: Candleholder
Size: 4" w x 6" h
Colors: wf-i-g-a-p-o-r
Catalog(s): 1972
Value: $12.00

TW-510 Aladdin
Item: Candleholder
Size: 9½" w x 6½" h
Colors: wf-i-g-a-p-o-r
Catalog(s): 1972
Value: $45.00

500S—El Greco 1.75
4½" x 6"
(W-G-A-P-O-I)

500L—El Greco 2.50
5" x 9½"
(W-G-A-P-O-I)

TW-500S El Greco (Short)
Item: Candleholder
Size: 4½" w x 6" h
Colors: wf-i-g-a-p-o-r
Catalog(s): 1972
Value: $12.00

TW-500L El Greco (Long)
Item: Candleholder
Size: 5" w x 9½" h
Colors: wf-i-g-a-p-o-r
Catalog(s): 1972
Value: $15.00

TW-503S Ravel(Short)
Item: Candleholder
Size: 4½" w x 6" h
Colors: wf-i-g-a-p-o-r
Catalog(s): 1972
Value: $15.00

CANDY JARS

TW-354 Bear
Item: Candy Jar
Size: 8" x 10½"
Colors: wf-i-g-a-p-o-r
Catalog(s): 1966, 1967, 1968, 1969,
1971, 1972, 1974, 1975
Value: $85.00
Note: Common name is Ranger Bear.

TW 354 Bear.................2.50
8 x 10½

TW 357 Elf 2.50
8½ x 8

TW-356 Elephant
Item: Candy Jar
Size: 6" x 9"
Colors: wf-i-g-a-p-o-r
Catalog(s): 1966, 1967, 1968, 1969, 1971,
1972, 1974, 1975
Value: $65.00
Note: Common name is Sailor Elephant.

TW-357 Elf
Item: Candy Jar
Size: 8½" x 8"
Colors: wf-i-g-a-p-o-r
Catalog(s): 1966, 1967, 1968, 1969, 1971, 1972, 1974, 1975
Value: $65.00

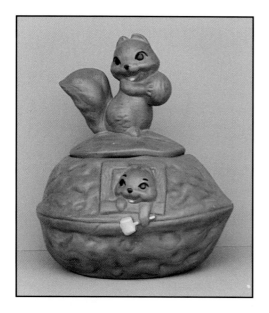

TW-353 Nut
Item: Candy Jar
Size: 8" x 9"
Colors: wf-i-g-a-p-o-r
Catalog(s): 1966, 1967, 1968,
1969, 1971, 1972, 1974, 1975
Value: $75.00

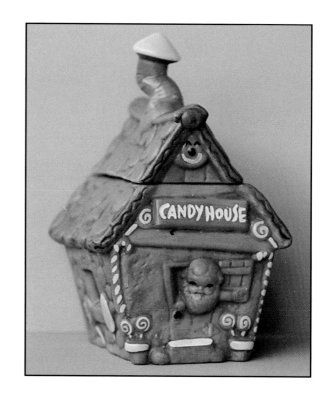

TW-351 Shack
Item: Candy Jar
Size: 6½" x 9½"
Colors: wf-i-g-a-p-o-r
Catalog(s): 1966, 1967, 1968,
1969, 1971, 1972, 1974, 1975
Value: $65.00

TW-359 Pot O'Candy
Item: Candy Jar
Size: 8" x 10"
Colors: wf-i-g-a-p-o-r
Catalog(s): 1971, 1972,
1974, 1975
Value: $65.00

TW-352 Shoe
Item: Candy Jar
Size: 10" x 10"
Colors: wf-i-g-a-p-o-r
Catalog(s): 1966, 1967, 1968,
1969, 1971
Value: $75.00

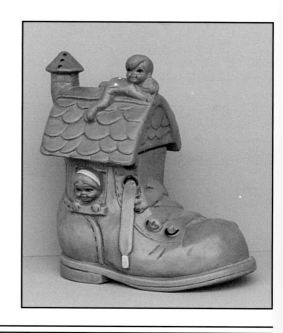

W-358 Train
em: Candy Jar
ze: 8" x 10"
olors: wf-i-g-a-p-o-r
atalog(s): 1967, 1968, 1969,
971, 1972, 1974, 1975
alue: $75.00

TW-350 Turtle
Item: Candy Jar
Size: 8" x 10"
Colors: wf-i-g-a-p-o-r
Catalog(s): 1966, 1967, 1968,
1969, 1971, 1972, 1974, 1975
Value: $85.00

CANISTER SET

No photos available for the following items.

TW-59 Cookie Bucket
Item: Canister Set
Size: 8" x 9"
Colors: wf-i-g-a-p-o-r
Catalog(s):
Value: $60.00
Note: Bucket canister set.

TW-60 Flour Bucket
Item: Canister Set
Size: 7" x 8"
Colors: wf
Catalog(s): 1963
Value: $50.00
Note: Bucket canister set.

TW-61 Sugar Bucket
Item: Canister Set
Size: 6" x 7"
Colors: wf
Catalog(s): 1963
Value: $40.00
Note: Bucket canister set.

TW-62 Coffee Bucket
Item: Canister Set
Size: 5" x 6"
Colors: wf
Catalog(s): 1963
Value: $30.00
Note: Bucket canister set.

CANISTERVILLE

TW-40 House (Cookies)
Item: Canister Set
Size: 8" x 12"
Colors: wf
Catalog(s): 1967, 1968
Value: $175.00
Note: Canisterville

TW-101 House (Flour)
Item: Canister Set
Size: 7" x 11"
Colors: wf
Catalog(s): 1967, 1968
Value: $125.00
Note: Canisterville

TW-102 House (Sugar)
Item: Canister Set
Size: 5" x 9"
Colors: wf
Catalog(s): 1967, 1968
Value: $95.00
Note: Canisterville

TW-103 House (Coffee)
Item: Canister Set
Size: 4" x 8"
Colors: wf
Catalog(s): 1967, 1968
Value: $75.00
Note: Canisterville

TW-104 House (Tea)
Item: Canister Set
Size: 3" x 7"
Colors: wf
Catalog(s): 1967, 1968
Value: $50.00
Note: Canisterville

TW-140 House (Salt & Pepper)
Item: Canister Set
Size: 5" h
Colors: wf
Catalog(s): 1967, 1968
Value: $75.00
Note: Canisterville. Note different design of salt and pepper.

CANISTER FARM

TW 41................3.50

TW 111................3.00

TW 112................2.50

TW 113................1.75

TW 114................1.25

TW 141................1.75 PR.

TW-41 Cookie Barn
Item: Canister Set
Size: 8" x 12"
Colors: wf-i-g-a-p-o-r
Catalog(s): 1967, 1968, 1969, 1971, 1972, 1974, 1975
Value: $80.00
Note: Canister Farm

TW-111 Flour Stable
Item: Canister Set
Size: 6" x 10"
Colors: wf-i-g-a-p-o-r
Catalog(s): 1967, 1968, 1969, 1971, 1972, 1974, 1975
Value: $65.00
Note: Canister Farm

TW-112 Sugar Dairy
Item: Canister Set
Size: 4" x 8"
Colors: wf-i-g-a-p-o-r
Catalog(s): 1967, 1968, 1969, 1971, 1972, 1974, 1975
Value: $55.00
Note: Canister Farm

TW-113 Coffee Coop
Item: Canister Set
Size: 4" x 6"
Colors: wf-i-g-a-p-o-r
Catalog(s): 1967, 1968, 1969, 1971, 1972, 1974, 1975
Value: $40.00
Note: Canister Farm

TW-114 Tea Sty
Item: Canister Set
Size: 3" x 5"
Colors: wf-i-g-a-p-o-r
Catalog(s): 1967, 1968, 1969, 1971, 1972, 1974, 1975
Value: $30.00
Note: Canister Farm

TW-141 Salt & Pepper
Item: Canister Set
Size: 4½" h
Colors: wf-i-g-a-p-o-r
Catalog(s): 1968, 1969, 1971, 1972, 1974, 1975
Value: $40.00   Note: Canister Farm

No photos available for the following items.

TW-58 Pot O' Cookies
Item: Canister Set
Size: 8" x 10"
Colors: wf-i-g-a-p-o-r
Catalog(s): 1971, 1972, 1974, 1975
Value: $40.00
Note: Pot O'Canisters

TW-122 Pot O' Sugar
Item: Canister Set
Size: 6" x 7"
Colors: wf-i-g-a-p-o-r
Catalog(s): 1971, 1972, 1974, 1975
Value: $30.00
Note: Pot O'Canisters

TW-124 Pot O' Tea
Item: Canister Set
Size: 4" x 5"
Colors: wf-i-g-a-p-o-r
Catalog(s): 1971, 1972, 1974, 1975
Value: $20.00
Note: Pot O'Canisters

TW-121 Pot O' Flour
Item: Canister Set
Size: 7" x 8"
Colors: wf-i-g-a-p-o-r
Catalog(s): 1971, 1972, 1974, 1975
Value: $35.00
Note: Pot O'Canisters

TW-123 Pot O' Coffee
Item: Canister Set
Size: 5" x 6"
Colors: wf-i-g-a-p-o-r
Catalog(s): 1971, 1972, 1974, 1975
Value: $25.00
Note: Pot O'Canisters

TW-158 Pot O' Salt & Pepper (Set)
Item: Canister Set
Size: 3½" h
Colors: wf-i-g-a-p-o-r
Catalog(s): 1971, 1972, 1974, 1975
Value: $30.00
Note: Pot O'Canisters

Cocktail Napkin
Holders

COCKTAIL NAPKIN HOLDERS

(Individually Boxed)

TW 450 ....1.75

TW 451 ....1.75

TW 452 ....1.75

TW 453 ....1.75

TW-450 Horse
Item: Cocktail Napkin Holder
Size: 6" h x 4" w
Colors: wf-i-g-a-p-o-r
Catalog(s): 1968, 1969, 1971
Value: $150.00

TW-451 Dog
Item: Cocktail Napkin Holder
Size: 6" h x 4" w
Colors: wf-i-g-a-p-o-r
Catalog(s): 1968, 1969, 1971
Value: $150.00

TW-452 Rabbit
Item: Cocktail Napkin Holder
Size: 6" h x 4" w
Colors: wf-i-g-a-p-o-r
Catalog(s): 1968, 1969, 1971
Value: $150.00

TW-453 Elephant
Item: Cocktail Napkin Holder
Size: 6" h x 4" w
Colors: wf-i-g-a-p-o-r
Catalog(s): 1968, 1969, 1971
Value: $150.00

Expanimals

EXPANIMALS

(Individually Boxed)

TW 125—POODLE ......5.00 set

CAN BE USED AS . . .

SERVERS

TW 126—KITTEN ....5.00 set

TW 127—CHIPMUNK ..5.00 set

PLANTERS

BOOK-ENDS

TW 526 ....3.50 pr.

TW 527 ....3.50 pr.
    (Not Pictured)

TW 525 ....3.50 pr.

TW 5—ADDITIONAL DIVIDERS FOR SERVERS ....75 ea.

TW-125 Poodle (set)
Item: Expanimal/Bookends
Size: approx. 7½" h
Colors: wf
Catalog(s): 1968
Value: $125.00
Note: This is a different version of the poodle design from others with the same name listed in the catalogs.

TW-126 Kitten (set)
Item: Expanimal/Bookends
Size: approx. 7½" h
Colors: wf
Catalog(s): 1968
Value: $125.00

TW-127 Chipmunk (set)
Item: Expanimal/Bookends
Size: approx. 7½" h
Colors: wf
Catalog(s): 1968
Value: $125.00

TW-5 Additional Dividers
Item: Expanimal
Colors: wf
Catalog(s): 1968, 1969
Value: $15.00

$\mathcal{F}$IGURINES

603—Cocker Spaniel 7" 2.50

602—Collie 7½" 3.00

607—Female Cat 9½" 3.00

TW-603 Cocker Spaniel
Item: Figurine
Size: 7" h
Colors: wf-g-i-hand painted
Catalog(s): 1972
Value: $50.00

TW-601 Hunting Dog
Item: Figurine
Size: 11" w
Colors: wf-g-i-hand painted
Catalog(s): 1972
Value: $85.00

TW-602 Collie
Item: Figurine
Size: 7½" h
Colors: wf-g-i-hand painted
Catalog(s): 1972
Value: $65.00

TW-607 Female Cat
Item: Figurine
Size: 9½" w
Colors: wf-g-i-hand painted
Catalog(s): 1972
Value: $75.00

TW-606 Male Cat
Item: Figurine
Size: 9" h
Colors: wf-g-i-hand painted
Catalog(s): 1972
Value: $75.00

605—Persian 8½" 3.50

TW-605 Persian
Item: Figurine
Size: 8½" h
Colors: wf-g-i-hand painted
Catalog(s): 1972
Value: $65.00

TW-604 Shaggy Dog
Item: Figurine
Size: 8" h
Colors: wf-g-i-hand painted
Catalog(s): 1972
Value: $65.00

Ice Buckets

TW-31 Bathing
Item: Ice Bucket
Size: 7½" x 16"
Colors: wf
Catalog(s): 1963, 1964, 1966
Value: $450.00

TW-32 Bottoms Up
Item: Ice Bucket
Size: 7½" x 14"
Colors: wf
Catalog(s): 1963, 1964, 1966,
1967, 1968, 1969, 1971
Value: $250.00

TW-30 Suspenders
Item: Ice Bucket
Size: 7½" x 14"
Colors: wf
Catalog(s): 1963, 1964, 1966, 1967, 1968, 1969, 1971
Value: $250.00

TW-33 With Jug
Item: Ice Bucket
Size: 7½" x 14"
Colors: wf
Catalog(s): 1963, 1964, 1966, 1967, 1968, 1969, 1971
Value: $350.00

LAMPS

TW-255 Squirrel
Item: Lamp
Size: approx 12" h
Colors: wf
Catalog(s): 1963, 1964, 1966, 1967, 1968
Value: $175.00

ACCENT LAMPS

TW 259 Monkey Lamp 4.00

TW 257 Hotei Lamp 4.00

TW 252 Cat & Fiddle 5.00

TW 258 Kitten Lamp 4.00

TW 260 Seal Lamp 4.00

TW-259 Monkey
Item: Lamp
Size: approx. 13" h
Colors: wf
Catalog(s): 1963, 1964, 1966,
1967, 1968
Value: $175.00

TW-257 Hotei
Item: Lamp
Size: approx. 12" h
Colors: wf
Catalog(s): 1963, 1964, 1966,
1967, 1968
Value: $175.00

TW-252 Cat & Fiddle
Item: Lamp
Size: approx. 11" h
Colors: wf
Catalog(s): 1963, 1964, 1966,
1967, 1968
Value: $175.00

TW-258 Kitten
Item: Lamp
Size: approx. 13" h
Colors: wf
Catalog(s): 1963, 1964, 1966,
1967, 1968
Value: $175.00

TW-260 Seal
Item: Lamp
Size: approx. 12" h
Colors: wf
Catalog(s): 1963, 1964, 1966,
1967, 1968
Value: $175.00

ACCENT LAMPS

TW 250 Bear 5.00

For Child's Room

TW 251 Rabbit 5.00

For Dens

TW 253 Raccoon 4.00

For Kitchens

TW 256 Elephant 4.00

Any Room in the House

TW 254 Bambi 4.00

TW-250 Bear
Item: Lamp
Size: approx. 12" h
Colors: wf
Catalog(s): 1963, 1964, 1966, 1967, 1968
Value: $175.00

TW-251 Rabbit
Item: Lamp
Size: approx. 12" h
Colors: wf
Catalog(s): 1963, 1964, 1966, 1967, 1968
Value: $175.00

TW-253 Raccoon
Item: Lamp
Size: approx. 12" h
Colors: wf
Catalog(s): 1964, 1966, 1967, 1968
Value: $175.00

TW-256 Elephant
Item: Lamp
Size: approx. 11" h
Colors: wf
Catalog(s): 1963, 1964, 1966, 1967, 1968
Value: $175.00

TW-254 Bambi
Item: Lamp
Size: approx. 11" h
Colors: wf
Catalog(s): 1963, 1964, 1966, 1967, 1968
Value: $175.00

Mugs

TW-504 Bear
Item: Mug
Size: 3¼" h
Colors: wf-i-g-a-p-o-r
Catalog(s): 1967, 1968, 1969
Value: $85.00

TW-505 Elephant
Item: Mug
Size: 3¼" h
Colors: wf-i-g-a-p-o-r
Catalog(s): 1967, 1968, 1969
Value: $85.00

TW-503 Kitten
Item: Mug
Size: 3¼" h
Colors: wf-i-g-a-p-o-r
Catalog(s): 1967, 1968, 1969
Value: $85.00

TW-502 Lamb
Item: Mug
Size: 3¼" h
Colors: wf-i-g-a-p-o-r
Catalog(s): 1967, 1968, 1969
Value: $85.00

TW-501 Owl
Item: Mug
Size: 3¼" h
Colors: wf-i-g-a-p-o-r
Catalog(s): 1967, 1968, 1969
Value: $85.00

Napkin Holders

TW-500 Puppy
Item: Mug
Size: 3¼" h
Colors: wf-i-g-a-p-o-r
Catalog(s): 1967, 1968, 1969
Value: $85.00

TW-480 Bambi
Item: Napkin Holder
Size: 6" h x 7" w
Colors: wf-i-g-a-p-o-r
Catalog(s): 1966, 1967, 1968,
1969, 1971, 1972, 1974, 1975
Value: $85.00

TW-478 Bear
Item: Napkin Holder
Size: 9" h x 4" w
Colors: wf-i-g-a-p-o-r
Catalog(s): 1966, 1967, 1968, 1969, 1971, 1972, 1974, 1975
Value: $75.00

TW-484 Butler
Item: Napkin Holder
Size: 7" h x 5" w
Colors: wf-i-g-a-p-o-r
Catalog(s): 1967, 1968, 1969, 1971
Value: $100.00

TW-479 Cow
Item: Napkin Holder
Size: 6" h x 7" w
Colors: wf-i-g-a-p-o-r
Catalog(s): 1966, 1967, 1968,
1969, 1971, 1972, 1974, 1975
Value: $85.00

TW-487 Dobbin
Item: Napkin Holder
Size: 7" h x 5" w
Colors: wf-i-g-a-p-o-r
Catalog(s): 1967, 1968, 1969,
1971, 1972, 1974, 1975
Value: $65.00

TW-471 Dutch Girl
Item: Napkin Holder
Size: 8½" h x 5½" w
Colors: wf-i-g-a-p-o-r
Catalog(s): 1966, 1967, 1968, 1969, 1971, 1972, 1974, 1975
Value: $75.00

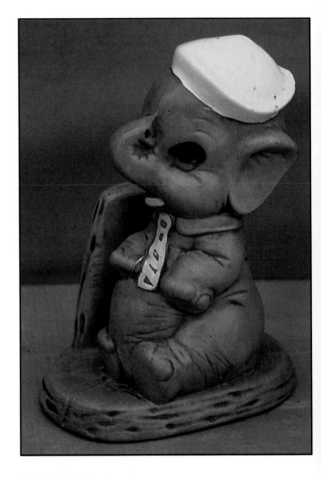

TW-486 Elephant
Item: Napkin Holder
Size: 7" h x 5" w
Colors: wf-i-g-a-p-o-r
Catalog(s): 1967, 1968, 1969, 1971, 1972, 1974, 1975
Value: $75.00

TW-476 Elf
Item: Napkin Holder
Size: 8" h x 5" w
Colors: wf-i-g-a-p-o-r
Catalog(s): 1966, 1967, 1968, 1969, 1971, 1972, 1974, 1975
Value: $85.00

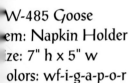
W-485 Goose
em: Napkin Holder
ze: 7" h x 5" w
olors: wf-i-g-a-p-o-r
atalog(s): 1967, 1968, 1969,
?71, 1972, 1974, 1975
'alue: $75.00

TW-475 Hotei
Item: Napkin Holder
Size: 8" h x 6" w
Colors: wf-i-g-a-p-o-r
Catalog(s): 1966, 1967, 1968,
1969, 1971, 1972, 1974, 1975
Value: $85.00

TW-482 Lamb
Item: Napkin Holder
Size: 7" h x 5" w
Colors: wf-i-g-a-p-o-r
Catalog(s): 1967, 1968, 1969,
1971, 1972, 1974, 1975
Value: $75.00

TW-472 Owl
Item: Napkin Holder
Size: 7" h x 5" w
Colors: wf-i-g-a-p-o-r
Catalog(s): 1966, 1967, 1968,
1969, 1971, 1972, 1974, 1975
Value: $65.00

TW-470 Persian Cat
Item: Napkin Holder
Size: 5½" h x 7" w
Colors: wf-i-g-a-p-o-r
Catalog(s): 1966, 1967, 1968,
1969, 1971, 1972, 1974, 1975
Value: $75.00

TW-474 Poodle
Item: Napkin Holder
Size: 7" h x 7" w
Colors: wf-i-g-a-p-o-r
Catalog(s): 1966, 1967, 1968,
1969, 1971, 1972, 1974, 1975
Value: $75.00

TW-473 Porky Pig
Item: Napkin Holder
Size: 8" h x 5" w
Colors: wf-i-g-a-p-o-r
Catalog(s): 1966, 1967, 1968,
1969, 1971, 1972, 1974, 1975
Value: $75.00

TW-488 Pot Bellied Stove
Item: Napkin Holder
Size: 7" h x 5" w
Colors: wf-i-g-a-p-o-r
Catalog(s): 1971, 1972, 1974, 1975
Value: $75.00

TW-483 Rooster
Item: Napkin Holder
Size: 7" h x 6" w
Colors: wf-i-g-a-p-o-r
Catalog(s): 1967, 1968, 1969,
1971, 1972, 1974, 1975
Value: $75.00

TW-481 Shack
Item: Napkin Holder
Size: 7" h x 7" w
Colors: wf-i-g-a-p-o-r
Catalog(s): 1966, 1967, 1968, 1969,
1971, 1972, 1974, 1975
Value: $65.00

ᴘLANTERS

TW 325 Bambi Planter 2.00

TW-325 Bambi
Item: Planter
Size: approx. 8" h
Colors: wf
Catalog(s): 1963, 1964
1966, 1967, 1968
Value: $50.00

TW-477 Squirrel
Item: Napkin Holder
Size: 8" h x 4" w
Colors: wf-i-g-a-p-o-r
Catalog(s): 1966, 1967, 1968, 1969,
1971, 1972, 1974, 1975
Value: $65.00

TW-328 Cat
Item: Planter
Size: approx. 8" h
Colors: wf
Catalog(s): 1963, 1964,
1966, 1967, 1968
Value: $50.00

TW 328 Cat Planter 2.00

TW-324 Bear
Item: Planter
Size: approx. 8" h
Colors: wf
Catalog(s): 1963, 1964,
1966, 1967, 1968
Value: $50.00

TW 327 Dog Planter 2.00

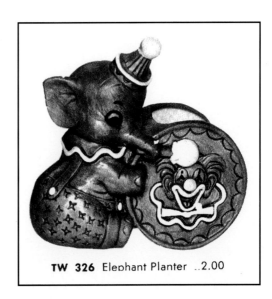

TW 326 Elephant Planter ..2.00

TW-327 Dog
Item: Planter
Size: approx. 8" h
Colors: wf
Catalog(s): 1963, 1964,
1966, 1967, 1968
Value: $50.00

TW-326 Elephant
Item: Planter
Size: approx. 8" h
Colors: wf
Catalog(s): 1963, 1964,
1966, 1967, 1968
Value: $50.00

Spoon Rests

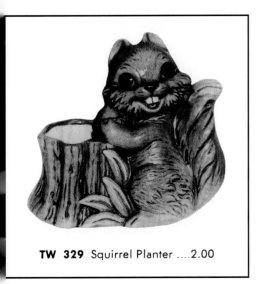

TW 329 Squirrel Planter 2.00

TW-329 Squirrel
Item: Planter
Size: approx. 8" h
Colors: wf
Catalog(s): 1963, 1964,
1966, 1967, 1968
Value: $50.00

TW-12 Bear
Item: Spoon Rest
Size: appox. 5" x 10"
Colors: wf-i-g-a-p-o-r
Catalog(s): 1964, 1966, 1967, 1968, 1969, 1971, 1972, 1974
Value: $40.00

TW-23 Cow
Item: Spoon Rest
Size: approx. 5" x 10"
Colors: wf-i-g-a-p-o-r
Catalog(s): 1966, 1967, 1968,
1969, 1971, 1972, 1974
Value: $40.00

TW-19 Dutch Girl
Item: Spoon Rest
Size: approx. 5" x 10"
Colors: wf-i-g-a-p-o-r
Catalog(s): 1966, 1967, 1968,
1969, 1971, 1972, 1974
Value: $40.00

TW-13 Elephant
Item: Spoon Rest
Size: approx. 5" x 10"
Colors: wf-i-g-a-p-o-r
Catalog(s): 1964, 1966, 1967,
1968, 1969, 1971, 1972, 1974
Value: $40.00

TW-10 Lamb
Item: Spoon Rest
Size: approx. 5" x 10"
Colors: wf-i-g-a-p-o-r
Catalog(s): 1964, 1966, 1967,
1968, 1969, 1971, 1972, 1974
Value: $40.00

TW 17 Elf 1.00

TW-17 Elf
Item: Spoon Rest
Size: approx. 5" x 10"
Colors: wf-i-g-a-p-o-r
Catalog(s): 1966, 1967,
1968, 1969, 1971,
1972, 1974
Value: $40.00

TW 21 Owl..........1.00

TW 15 Kitten 1.00

TW 20 Hotei 1.00

TW-21 Owl
Item: Spoon Rest
Size: approx. 5" x 10"
Colors: wf-i-g-a-p-o-r
Catalog(s): 1966, 1967, 1968,
1969, 1971, 1972, 1974
Value: $40.00

TW-15 Kitten
Item: Spoon Rest
Size: approx. 5" x 10"
Colors: wf-i-g-a-p-o-r
Catalog(s): 1966, 1967, 1968,
1969, 1971, 1972, 1974
Value: $40.00

TW-20 Hotei
Item: Spoon Rest
Size: approx. 5" x 10"
Colors: wf-i-g-a-p-o-r
Catalog(s): 1966, 1967, 1968,
1969, 1971, 1972, 1974
Value: $40.00

TW 14 Pig 1.00

TW 16 Poodle.... .....1.00

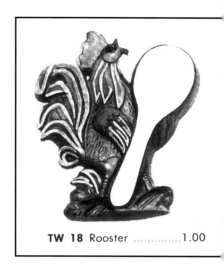

TW 18 Rooster 1.00

TW-14 Pig
Item: Spoon Rest
Size: approx. 5" x 10"
Colors: wf-i-g-a-p-o-r
Catalog(s): 1966, 1967, 1968,
1969, 1971, 1972, 1974
Value: $40.00

TW-16 Poodle
Item: Spoon Rest
Size: approx. 5" x 10"
Colors: wf-i-g-a-p-o-r
Catalog(s): 1966, 1967, 1968,
1969, 1971, 1972, 1974
Value: $40.00

TW-18 Rooster
Item: Spoon Rest
Size: approx. 5" x 10"
Colors: wf-i-g-a-p-o-r
Catalog(s): 1966, 1967, 1968,
1969, 1971, 1972, 1974
Value: $40.00

TW 11 Squirrel 1.00

TW 22 Turtle...........1.00

TW-11 Squirrel
Item: Spoon Rest
Size: approx. 5" x 10"
Colors: wf-i-g-a-p-o-r
Catalog(s): 1964, 1966, 1967,
1968, 1969, 1971, 1972, 1974
Value: $40.00

TW-22 Turtle
Item: Spoon Rest
Size: approx. 5" x 10"
Colors: wf-i-g-a-p-o-r
Catalog(s): 1966, 1967, 1968,
1969, 1971, 1972, 1974
Value: $40.00

TW 220—COW AND BULL SET ....2.50 set

TW-220 Cow and Bull Set
Item: Sugar & Creamer
Size: approx. 5" x 6"
Colors: wf-g-i
Catalog(s): 1968, 1969, 1971, 1972, 1974
Value: $200.00

Sugar Bowls & Creamers

TW-221 Hen and Rooster Set
Item: Sugar & Creamer
Size: approx. 5" x 6"
Colors: wf-g-i
Catalog(s): 1968, 1969, 1971, 1972, 1974
Value: $200.00

I CAN'T BEAR NOT TO BE LOVED

Talking Pictures

TW-439 Teddy Bear
Item: Talking Picture
Size: 11" h x 7" w
Colors: wf-g-i-a-p-o-r
Catalog(s): 1966, 1967, 1968, 1969
Value: $110.00

TW 434 ....1.75

TW 432 ....1.75

TW 436 ....1.75

TW 437 ....1.75

TW-434 Bear
Item: Talking Picture
Size: 11" h x 7" w
Colors: wf-g-i-a-p-o-r
Catalog(s): 1966, 1968, 1969
Value: $110.00

TW-432 Squirrel
Item: Talking Picture
Size: 11" h x 7" w
Colors: wf-g-i-a-p-o-r
Catalog(s): 1966, 1967, 1968, 1969
Value: $110.00

TW-437 Cow
Item: Talking Picture
Size: 7" h x 11" w
Colors: wf-g-i-a-p-o-r
Catalog(s): 1966, 1967, 1968, 1969
Value: $110.00

TW-436 Elephant
Item: Talking Picture
Size: 11" h x 7" w
Colors: wf-g-i-a-p-o-r
Catalog(s): 1966, 1967, 1968, 1969
Value: $110.00

TW-438 Hotei
Item: Talking Picture
Size: 11" h x 7" w
Colors: wf-g-i-a-p-o-r
Catalog(s): 1966, 1967, 1968, 1969
Value: $110.00

TW-433 Persian Cat
Item: Talking Picture
Size: 11" h x 7" w
Colors: wf-g-i-a-p-o-r
Catalog(s): 1966, 1967, 1968, 1969
Value: $110.00

TW-435 Shoe
Item: Talking Picture
Size: 10" h x 11" w
Colors: wf-g-i-a-p-o-r
Catalog(s): 1966, 1967, 1968, 1969
Value: $110.00

TW 438 ....1.75

TW 433 ....1.75

TW 430 ....1.75

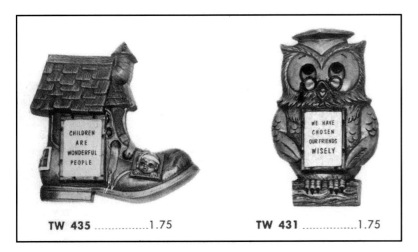

TW 435 .... 1.75   TW 431 .... 1.75

TW-430 Shack
Item: Talking Picture
Size: 10½" h x 10½" w
Colors: wf-g-i-a-p-o-r
Catalog(s): 1966, 1967, 1968, 1969
Value: $110.00

TW-431 Owl
Item: Talking Picture
Size: 11" h x 7" w
Colors: wf-g-i-a-p-o-r
Catalog(s): 1966, 1967, 1968, 1969
Value: $110.00

Wall Planters

TW-300 Bear
Item: Wall Planter (Animal Head)
Size: approx. 5½" h
Colors: wf
Catalog(s): 1963, 1964
Value: $100.00

TW-304 Elephant
Item: Wall Planter (Animal Head)
Size: approx. 5½" h
Colors: wf
Catalog(s): 1963, 1964
Value: $100.00

TW-301 Lamb
Item: Wall Planter (Animal Head)
Size: approx. 5½" h
Colors: wf
Catalog(s): 1963, 1964
Value: $100.00

TW-302 Rabbit
Item: Wall Planter (Animal Head)
Size: approx. 5½" h
Colors: wf
Catalog(s): 1963, 1964
Value: $100.00

TW-303 Puppy
Item: Wall Planter (Animal Head)
Size: approx. 5½" h
Colors: wf
Catalog(s): 1963, 1964
Value: $100.00

THE END
(Not By a Long Shot!!)

I have enjoyed writing this book about Don & Norma Winton. You cannot write about Don without understanding that Norma is the love of his life and his inspiration for creating things beautiful. In writing it I have learned about a man that has truly been blessed. His generosity and humility have been matched only by the God-given talent that is evident in all his creations.

In deciding what to include in this book I had also to decide what to eliminate. Many of you will doubtless be disappointed that some things were eliminated and other items were included. Don has created and designed well over 15,000 items in his lifetime and the number is growing daily. You may be fortunate enough to own one of his pencil drawings. You can find his work at the county fair in a sipper bottle or the bust of President Ronald Reagan in the memorial library. You may call your best friend on the Mickey Mouse telephone or get a cookie out of the Bob's Big Boy cookie jar he designed. His designs are all around us and daily I am surprised at the things he has designed and had a hand in developing. The ideas he has for future projects would take us well into the next century. His art work will last well beyond that.

As the final chapter, I am going to show the variety of his designs that we are all interested in and list some items that intrigue me. The value of these items will be left open for discussion for future books. I will make a prediction for the future however. The name of Don Winton will be long remembered in American art and the value of his creations will continue to rise. Perhaps with the exchange of information through the collectors and antique dealers we can continue to gather and preserve more information about this great man and the many wonderful designs he has created.

Christmas Items

Merry Xmas Planter
4" x 15", $40.00.

Marking on bottom of sleigh.

Santa Sleigh and Reindeer
sleigh 7" long, $150.00,
reindeer 7" high, $75.00.

Santa Plate
14" diameter, $50.00.
(There is also a small Santa plate approximately
7" – value $30.00.)

Planters

Golf Bag
7", $50.00.

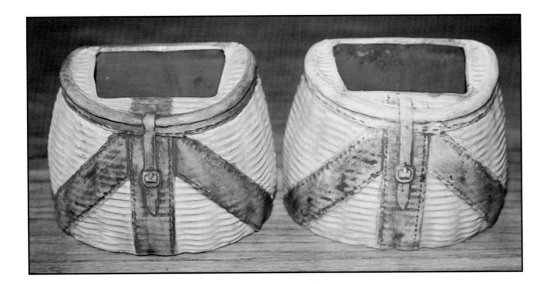

Fisherman Basket Planter
6" h, $60.00.

Pipe Planter
5" h, $50.00.

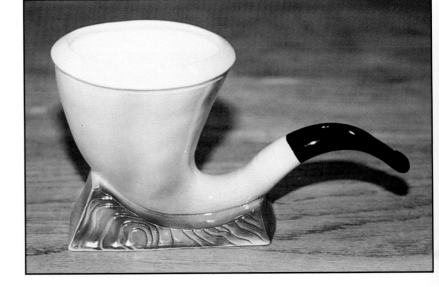

Bamboo Planter
12" h, $45.00.

Coins

Abraham Lincoln
2", .999 fine silver, $40.00.
(This was made as a sample and given
as gifts to friends of Don.)

Gerald Ford
2", .999 fine silver, $35.00.
(One of a series of four Republi-
can Presidential coins manufactured for the Reagan Library. The
other Presidents were Nixon,
Bush, and Reagan.)

Marines landing
on Iwo Jima
2", .999 fine silver, $35.00.
(Made for company that
sold them on the El Toro Air
Base in California.)

Kitchen & Tableware

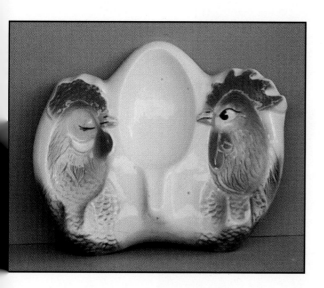

Rooster Spoon Holder
8", $80.00.

Pig Toothpick Dispenser
5", $60.00.

Rooster Teapot
10" h, $125.00.

Spur and Rope Mug
5" h, $30.00.

Garlic Holder
4½" h , $40.00.

Garlic Salt and Pepper
3" h, $20.00 ea.

Chip n Dip Bowl
5" x 8", $75.00.

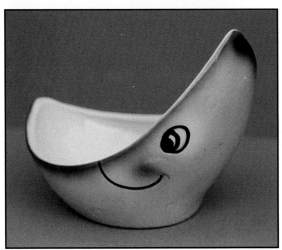

Barrel Salt and Pepper
3", $50.00.
(Part of the Artist Palette dish line.)

Angel Candy Jar
8", $40.00.
(Found as angel in Alberta
Molds.)

Archival photo of vase and
bowls designed for Vohann of
San Juan Capistrano.

Hop-a-Long Cassidy Cookie Jar
15", $3,500.00+.
(This is the only one known to exist with two
guns. The jar with one gun was issued in a limited
edition of 250.)

Don Winton at the National Cookie Jar Convention in Tennessee working on the 1997 Leprechaun cookie jar.

Figurines

Shepherd Boy
8" h, $75.00.

Flower Figurine
7", $85.00.

Small Standing Gazelle
8" h, $25.00.
(Designed by Don for Florence Ceramics.)

Large Standing Gazelle
12" h, $50.00.
(Designed by Don for Florence Ceramics.)

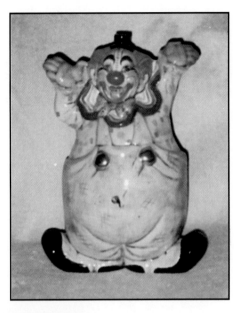

Clown Figure
20", $150.00.

Humpty Dumpty
Figurine
6½", $125.00.

Astronaut
30", $400.00.
(Made by Don and Ross for display,
only one known to exist.)

Angel
8", $100.00.

Football Figurine
8", $80.00.
(Designed for Duncan Royale of
Fullerton.)

Bruce Winton
7", one of a kind.

Balinese Dancers
18", $1,500.00 ea.
(Don would like to see these if they still exist.)

Dancer
18", $1,500.00.
(Don would like to know
if this still exists.)

Unicorn
22", $800.00.
(Made from red terra-cotta clay, only three
known to exist.)

Ibex
12" x 20", $250.00.

Clocks

Panda Bear
11" x 5", $85.00.

Poodle
13½" x 5", $100.00.

Rubber Toys

Donald Duck Soap Boat
6¾" l x 5¾" h x 5" w, $125.00.

Noah's Ark
10" x 7", $100.00.

Tug Boat
4" x 7", $40.00.

I must end this book with the most expensive cookie jar most of us have ever heard about. Don was asked to do a one-of-a-kind jar which was to be a bust of him and Norma. It was auctioned off at the National Cookie Jar Convention and brought a whopping $7,900.00. The lucky man who bought it is long-time Winton collector Charlie Snyder of Kansas. Although I am sure that jar will never hold cookies it will certainly be treasured by future generations of art lovers.

During the writing of this book, Don and Norma in their wonderful way of surprising me, said they were once again taking over the ownership of Twin Winton. They have concluded the deal and are now the sole owner of Twin Winton. He has already created six new jars that are now on the market in a limited quantity of 500 pieces each. These beautiful creations will be airbrushed with some hand decoration. I guess retirement is not something that Don and Norma will ever consider because Don has too much creativity and energy to sit still. Just as Don's mom sat him down at a table in 1924 to keep him busy, Norma has once again sat him down with a lump of clay and told him to make something.

The Twin Winton Collector's Club was formed to help keep track of Don's designs and to share information that will be helpful to us all in our search for his treasures. It is now on the Internet and has a quarterly newsletter. For more information look for us at www.twinwinton.com or write to Mike Ellis, 266 Rose Lane, Costa Mesa, CA 92627. I know you will find the information in this book helpful in your search for treasures and thank you for helping to preserve the history these wonderful pieces represent.

DEDICATION

During the writing of this book my 93-year-old grandfather died. I found this picture of him at the house he built and lived in for 50 years. The memories that he gave me, I am sure, contribute to the love of antiques and the joy I find in looking at and collecting Don Winton pieces. One of his favorite sayings was "You've got to find the joy of life rather than feel sorry for yourself." Well, Grandpa, here's to the joy of life.

A hundred years from now
It will not matter
What your bank account was
Or the sort of house you lived in,
Or the kind of car you drove,
But the world may be
A little different because
You were important in
The life of a little boy

I have this saying on my desk because Grandpa was important in my life as a little boy.

ABOUT THE AUTHOR

My name is Michael Leon Ellis, I am 47 years old as of the writing of this book, and in 1990 I had no idea who Don Winton was or that he would have anything to do with me. I have been self employed since 1986, married to Cindy since 1974, the father of three children Jennifer 18, Rebecca 15, John 14, and I tend to be a collector. My wife says "packrat." I have never before written a book, nor did I ever intend to be an author. In 1991 my father-in-law was telling me about this sculptor that went to his Sunday school class at our church. I was in need of a sculptor for my paper casting business and so I called Don. My first meeting was all business as far as I was concerned. I should be in and out in 15 minutes, I thought. I had no idea about the charming gentleman I was about to meet. After two hours of wonderful stories, incredible art, watching him take a lump of clay and create a whimsical animal that would not exist without him, I was hooked. I now understand the verse out of the Bible that says, "Yet, O Lord, you are our Father, we are the clay, you are the potter; we are all the work of your hand." Isaiah 64:8. Don had already affected my life in just two hours. Growing up in Southern California I found out I had gone to school with his nephew Kirk, was given one of his cookie jar designs when I got married, and my children had earned trophies of his designs as they were growing up. I was sharing this information with Joyce Roerig and she encouraged me to start taking notes. As I collected more of Don's cookie jars and started looking through boxes in his garage I was encouraged to share this information in a book. I mailed Lisa Stroup at Collector Books a chapter and some pictures I had found, within four weeks Collector Books sent me a contract and this book is the result. This book is by no means a comprehensive coverage of all of Don's work. I included some of the things that I needed and will possibly write another follow up book to this one if the collectors need the information. I am currently working on helping him to organize his original pencil drawings and am also working on registering some of his

major works with the Smithsonian Institute in Washington DC. I have gone to great efforts to verify the information in this book by more than one source, and hope that as you go treasure hunting for Don's designs you will find it useful.

I am gathering information for the Twin Winton Collector Club which I started and would love to share your information with other collectors. I am also excited that Don and Norma Winton have restarted Twin Winton and are coming out with new designs. Please feel free to call, write, or e-mail me with any questions you might have about this book or Don Winton designs.

Michael L. Ellis
Twin Winton Collector Club
266 Rose Lane
Costa Mesa, CA 92627
phone: (714) 646-7112
fax: (714) 645-4919
e-mail: ellis5@pacbell.net
Twin Winton Collector Club address on the Internet: www.twinwinton.com